A Creative Church
The Arts and a Century of Renewal
REVISED PRINTING

Todd Smith, MFA
Chair, Department of Studio and Digital Arts,
Director, Liberty University Art Gallery

Cover design: Carson Ford
Interior design: RJS Design Studio

Cover image by Carson Ford

www.kendallhunt.com
Send all inquiries to:
4050 Westmark Drive
Dubuque, IA 52004-1840

Copyright © 2014 by Anthony Todd Smith

ISBN 978-1-4652-8320-7

Kendall Hunt Publishing Company has the exclusive rights to reproduce this work,
to prepare derivative works from this work, to publicly distribute this work,
to publicly perform this work and to publicly display this work.

All rights reserved. No part of this publication may be reproduced,
stored in a retrieval system, or transmitted, in any form or by any
means, electronic, mechanical, photocopying, recording, or otherwise,
without the prior written permission of the copyright owner.

Printed in the United States of America

*To my wife, Melody, and my sons
Caleb and Luke*

Acknowledgements

I would like to thank my father and mother, who provided a Christian home for my siblings, Tammy, Randy and me. Speaking of my siblings, many thanks to them for their prayers and words of encouragement.

To Dr. James and Mary Taylor, who are with the Lord, I am truly grateful to them for nurturing my wife Melody to be a godly woman. I'm blessed to be part of her family. Dr. Taylor was an educator, mentor and friend.

My sons Caleb and Luke were a real blessing during the work for this book, providing times of humor and encouragement.

Four pioneers of the arts renewal movement provided feedback and advice for the first printing of this book: Bill Drake, Dr. Frank Fortunato, Dr. Byron Spradlin, and Dr. Colin Harbinson. For this revised printing, the voices of eight other pioneers have been added: Makoto Fujimura, Dr. Jeremy Begbie, Dr. John Franklin, Sandra Bowden, Keith Thibodeaux, Chuck Neighbors, Steve Scott, and Ralph Carmichael. I'm truly grateful for their time and encouragement and for all they've done to help inform this book.

Dr. Shaun Henson has been a sounding board for my musings for many years now, and encouraged me to write this book.

Many thanks to the Grove Center for the Arts & Media for working with us on the use of Dr. Colin Harbinson's article.

It is a privilege to serve with the faculty of the School of Communication and Creative Arts. Thanks also go to Dr. Norman Mintle, Dean of the School of Communication and Creative Arts, as well as Scott Hayes, Associate Dean.

Many thanks to the team at Kendall Hunt – Linda Chapman, Curtis Ross, Rachel Simpson and Carson Ford.

Special thanks to Dr. Don Alban and P.J. Campbell.

CONTENTS

Introduction IX

1. Setting the Stage: Late Nineteenth-Century Developments 11

2. Voices of Renewal 21

    Pioneer Creative: Dr. Colin Harbinson 35

    Pioneer Creative: Jeremie Begbie 43

3. Theatre 45

    Pioneer Creative: Chuck Neighbors 57

4. Music 61

    Pioneer Creative: Bill Drake 77

    Pioneer Creative: Dr. Frank Fortunato 79

    Pioneer Creative: Ralph Carmichael 81

5. Visual Arts 85

    Pioneer Creative: Sandra Bowden 101

    Pioneer Creative: Makoto Fujimura 105

6. Dance 107

    Pioneer Creative: Keith and Kathy Thibodeaux 117

7. Intersections: Theology, Education, Arts 119

8. A Snapshot: Congregations, Denominations, and the Arts 125

9. Global Arts Networks and Renewal 135

    Pioneer Creative: Rev. Dr. Byron Spradlin 149

    Pioneer Creative: Steve Scott 151

    Pioneer Creative: John Franklin 157

ENDNOTES 167

BIBLIOGRAPHY 183

INDEX 197

Introduction

The work for this book began in 1998, but is also the culmination of many years of involvement in related art activities. In a very real sense, my first exposure to the arts began at home. Dad was an entrepreneur with an insatiable bent for learning, experimentation, and a desire to have his own company. Along the way, he tried his hand at numerous ventures, including making small-scale sculptures, which I watched with great interest. After years of hard work, he finally established a contracting business. Mom loved to sing and participated in church choir and also a small group that included her sister and a friend that traveled locally and would sing at various church functions.

In fact, the church our family attended had quite a few Creatives. Along with the customary share of seasonal plays, gospel singing groups, and cantatas, all members were encouraged to use their skills for God. The youth were also actively encouraged to exhibit their talents through an annual art competition that began locally and culminated on the national level. Categories included areas such as drama, creative writing, visual art, voice, and instrumental. As a teenager during the 70s, I remember when various music composed by the Jesus movement Creatives found its way into our youth meetings. These songs seemed to speak the words of the gospel in a fresh way accompanied by a sound that was "now." Initially known as Christian rock or praise music, it was welcomed or scorned by people across the country. I sensed something was different and powerful about the music and grew to enjoy it.

Interest in art followed in college in the early 80s, where I studied religion and began investigating the intersection of theology, culture, and the arts after reading Francis Schaeffer's book *How Should We Then Live*. On a practical level, involvement in the campus drama group, shooting video, painting large-scale murals for campus events, and creating yearbook covers provided outlets for artistic expression. It was also during this time that I began sculpting and drawing to illustrate occasional messages in church. In the late 80's Frank

Gabelein's book *The Christian, the Arts and the Truth* would play a key role in helping further shape my understanding of art and culture and the role of the Creative. By the mid-90s, I completed a second bachelors and MFA in Visual Art in preparation for teaching.

It was also in the late 80s and the decade following that I began investigating the influence of Creatives who were helping shape Christianity through art forms such as music, visual arts, literature, theatre, ballet, and dance. Creatives had developed galleries, festivals, concerts, conferences, and schools that were focused on the arts from a decidedly Christian perspective. While some were local in nature, others were national and international in scope. Christians in the Visual Arts, Ballet Magnificat! and Christians in the Theater Arts are examples of arts organizations that have gained national status. A common thread among these groups, as expressed in organizational vision statements, is to glorify God and engage culture through a renewal of artistic expression.

This book is not intended to be an exhaustive treatment of the movement, but rather a popular approach to the topic. In many ways, this effort is like an impressionist painting, we have to step back a bit to see the big picture. I have attempted, to the best of my ability, to cover the most important background developments beginning in the late nineteenth and early twentieth century to the present that gave rise to what I believe has been a century of arts renewal in the church.

ONE

Setting the Stage:
Late Nineteenth-Century Developments

"The interest in the study of art in its various branches being one
that is growing, and extending to every town and hamlet in the country."
—JOHN HEYL VINCENT, 1885

John Heyl Vincent, a Methodist Episcopal minister, was also a speaker, teacher, publisher and author. He created a summer camp in Chautauqua, New York.
©Corbis

Several late nineteenth-century developments would set the stage for the growing inclusion of the arts in American Christianity in the twentieth century. This set against a backdrop of the American Protestant churches' long history of limiting the use of the arts in congregational life, music being the general exception. With roots reaching back to the Protestant Reformation, this propensity to prohibit most artistic expression in congregational life would experience a transformation. One of the major advances for arts renewal within the church took place a quarter century earlier in New York. In 1874, John Heyl Vincent, a Methodist Episcopal minister, along with businessman Lewis Miller, created a summer camp in Chautauqua, New York, with the goal of training Sunday school teachers. A creative in his own right, Vincent was a speaker, teacher, publisher, and author who wrote books on various topics such as history, education, and theology. Over the years, thousands of people attended the summer Chautauqua Institute in New York as well as the numerous Chautauquas that sprang up in various states. People traveled by car, train, horse, and carriage to attend. Eventually, traveling Chautauquas would take the experience to villages and towns throughout the nation.

Chautauqua Society of Fine Arts

Early on, Vincent developed a broad-based experience that would cater to specific spiritual and educational needs of the laity. Courses were offered in a wide variety of arts. For example, by 1885, the Chautauqua Society of Fine Arts was established and directed by Frank Fowler who was assisted by Jeanette Gilder, the editor of "The Critic."[1] Classes were offered, according to Vincent "in elementary drawing; free-hand drawing and perspective; figure drawing from life; painting in water-colors; painting in oil; crayon portraits; crayon drawing."[2]

Vincent also saw a growing need for training based on "the interest in the study of art in its various branches being one that is growing, and extending to every town and hamlet in the country."[3] Vincent's commitment to the idea is evidenced by the construction of facilities at the Chautauqua Institute to accommodate instruction in fine art. The learning that occurred was then disseminated in churches and communities nationwide.

Denominations that were represented were typically Protestant and included Baptist, Congregational, Disciples, Lutheran, Methodist-Episcopal, Methodist Episcopal South, Friends, Presbyterian, United Brethren, United Presbyterian, Protestant Episcopal, Reformed Episcopal, Cumberland Presbyterian, Wesleyan Methodist, Evangelical Association, Free Will Baptist, and others.[4]

Sousa at Chautauqua; 1925
Courtesy of Library of Congress

The arts were regularly integrated into the schedule of presentations given during the summer as well. Frank Beard, a widely known illustrator and chalk talk artist, often appeared on stage as a presenter at Chautauqua. Concerts and singing schools, so popular at this time, were also held. W.F. Sherwin, who

Fisk Jubilee Singers
Courtesy of Library of Congress

studied under Lowell Mason, was a noted composer, hymn writer and musician who worked at Chautauqua as the first music director. Sherwin later worked at the New England Conservatory of Music.[5] Other musicians involved early on at Chautauqua included John Phillip Sousa, Tullius C. O'Kane, Phillip Paul Bliss, Eben Tourjee, Mary A. Lathbury, and The Fisk Jubilee Singers.

Fisk Jubilee Singers

In 1871, the Fisk Jubilee Singers began a tour to raise money for financially strapped Fisk University, one of the first institutions in the nation to offer educational opportunities to black students. The singers performed in cities throughout the United States, and eventually for President Ulysses S. Grant. They also toured Europe and performed for a number of dignitaries, including Queen Victoria. Their work in the United States and abroad helped break down racial stereotypes and set the stage for pioneering Creatives like Charles Albert Tindley and Thomas Andrew Dorsey, and for the growth of the arts in African American life and culture.

Singing Schools

Just as Chautauqua was part of the Sunday school reform movement, singing schools, which dated back to the eighteenth century, were meant to reform church music, worship services and educate churchgoers. In these courses, teachers would set up local ten day schools that provided music education and were tailored to meet the artistic needs of interested individuals from the community by providing flexible times for learning.[6]

The fundamentals of the shape note music system were taught, as well as music theory, leading and sight-reading with a culminating public performance of the art form. Once students gained enough knowledge of the system, they could then offer lessons of their own. Normal schools would eventually spring up throughout the rural communities of the nation offering protracted training for traveling music teachers who represented a music publisher's products, such as song books and pamphlets. These products, featuring recognized hymns as well as new gospel songs were used regularly in singing schools. Often one of the main public attractions in communities, singing schools were held in various states such as Mississippi, Alabama, Texas, South Carolina, Georgia, Arkansas, and North Carolina.[7]

> **Songbooks and pamphlets featuring recognized hymns as well as new gospel songs were used regularly in singing schools.**

Camp Meetings, Revivalism, and the Arts

While the Chautauqua provided an environment for education and appreciation of a broad range of the arts, evangelical camp meetings provided an important, almost exclusive, context for one form of art--musical expression. An affinity had existed for some time before the turn of the century between camp meetings, music and Creatives.

Revivals and camp meetings, so prevalent at the turn of the century, were held throughout the nation and provided fertile ground for gospel songs. While the main purpose of these gatherings was evangelistic, they provided an environment for talented Creatives to present a variety of musical genres

Fannie Crosby was one of the most well-known hymn writers of the late nineteenth century. Courtesy of Library of Congress

and styles such as solos, quartets, and choirs, accompanied by both standard and experimental instruments. Ira Sankey and Fannie Crosby epitomized the influence of the Creative in Christianity at this time.

Sankey was born 1840 in Edinburg, Pennsylvania and worked for a time for the United States government after the Civil War. After hearing him direct singing at a YMCA convention, Dwight L. Moody asked Sankey to consider working with him. Sankey accepted the offer to work with the evangelist and went on to become one of the best known song leaders and composers of his day, eventually writing 1,200 gospel tunes. Among his best-known songs were "The Ninety and Nine," "There'll Be No Dark Valley," "A Shelter in the Time of Storm," and "Faith is the Victory."[8]

Fannie Crosby, who lost her sight in youth due to an ill-prescribed treatment, was one of the most prolific hymn writers of the late nineteenth century. As a teenager, she attended the New York Institute for the Blind and eventually became a teacher there. She wrote more than 9,000 hymns, many used by Ira Sankey in D.L. Moody's crusades and sung in churches throughout America. Some of her best-known songs were "Blessed Assurance," "All the Way My Savior Leads Me," "To God Be the Glory," "Pass Me Not, O Gentle Savior," and "Jesus Keep Me Near the Cross."[9]

By the dawn of the twentieth century, millions of people in the nation had been impacted by revival services and camp meetings. At the same time, many came to love and appreciate the aesthetic and variety of musical art forms presented in evangelistic gatherings, which appealed directly to their emotional and spiritual needs.

Theological and Philosophical Influences

If a function of evangelicalism was reaching the souls of the population through artistic media like voice and instrumentation, then it would be for colleges, universities and seminaries interested in the intersection of art, theology and culture to broach the appeal to the intellect. In 1898, Abraham Kuyper delivered the Stone Lectures at Princeton Theological Seminary. Kuyper was a renowned Reformed theologian, scholar, author, journalist, and statesman, who, by 1905, became the Prime Minister of the Netherlands. Kuyper's lectures dealt with world view and the Christian's responsibility to engage culture on all levels, covering Calvinism's impact on life, religion, politics, science, the future, and, of particular interest here, its impact on art.[10]

Alexander Hall, Princeton Theological Seminary
Courtesy of Library of Congress

By including art as a sphere of Christian influence, and this among some of the leading theologians and intellectuals of his day, Kuyper gave legitimacy to its theological and cultural significance. He dealt with art again in his book *Wisdom and Wonder: Common*

Grace in Science and Art, covering the topics of wonder, beauty, glory, creativity, and worship. Kuyper had a far-reaching impact on reformed theology, education and philosophy in America and other countries influencing prominent Christian philosophers such as Nicholas Wolterstorff, Calvin Seerveld, Hans Rookmaaker, and Francis Schaeffer.

Catholic Liturgical Renewal

Other faith traditions were experiencing reform at this time as well. Among Catholics, the Liturgical Movement, initially an outgrowth of European monastic life, had been gradually shaping new attitudes about worship since the mid-nineteenth century. The pioneering work of Virgil Michel played a significant role in shaping the move for liturgical renewal in America. Among the main tenets of the movement was an effort to include congregational participation and expressions of worship within the liturgy. The movement laid the groundwork for significant changes that would take place in all levels of the Catholic Church during the twentieth century, especially in relation to the arts. Within the first half of the twentieth century, Catholic art was influenced by visionaries such as Maurice Lavanoux and arts organizations that were formed including the Liturgical Arts Society,[11] the Catholic Art Association, Pius X School of Liturgical Music and the Society for the Renewal of Christian Art, as well as a number of books, journals, conferences, and educational programs.

First Christian Church,
Columbus, Indiana
Designed by Eero Saarinen
Courtesy of Library of Congress

Sacred Space

Houses of worship are one of the most visible evidences of the Christian faith and provide sacred space for community, worship and spiritual growth. A number of styles informed the American architectural landscape before the beginning of the twentieth century. The Creatives who designed the churches of the new century reevaluated those of the nineteenth century, and, either denied, affirmed or blended the styles and assumptions that gave rise to these structures. Much of this was based on developing attitudes over the century about the church and its role in all levels of society. Catholic, Protestant and Orthodox churches were influenced by the liturgical movement as well, examining how interior and exterior spaces could most effectively incorporate the tenets of the liturgy in the modern world.

Dawn of a New Century: Dawn of a New Era

The twentieth century began with great optimism that a Christian society could be advanced in American culture. Developments in communication, entertainment, travel and technology, while fledgling at this stage, would expand rapidly and be used to shape the culture over the next century. As the social reforms of the Civil War continued to be implemented, other causes were advancing related to education, social concerns and politics. The Industrial Revolution had increased the wealth of the country while at the same time creating large urban populations. In the theological sphere, several factors helped set the stage for the growth of the arts in American Christianity, both Protestant and Catholic. Among Protestants, disputes about the inerrancy of scripture, Darwinism and the social gospel led to continued division of the Fundamentalist and Progressive camps.

> **At the dawn of the new century, the environment was ripe for reform on many levels. . . .**

Many saw American culture as an expression of Christianity, with various elements potentially aiding in the progress of civilization and righting past wrongs. Others interpreted facets of culture as diametrically opposed to what true Christianity should be. Society, it was believed, needed salvation at almost all levels. The evangelistic crusades and the growth of the Holiness, Evangelical and Pentecostal movements epitomized this concern. Visionaries representing a wide spectrum of the society set about reforming culture according to individualized interpretations of Christianity and institutions through which to express their agendas. At the dawn of the new century, the environment was ripe for reform on many levels, setting the stage for the growth and renewal of the arts in American and set the stage for what would become a worldwide movement.

TWO

Voices of Renewal

"To every movement, then, toward the restoration of diplomatic relations
between religion and art, the church must give her earnest support."
—RALPH ADAMS CRAM, 1914

William H.P. Faunce, president of Brown University in 1905.
Courtesy of Library of Congress

Throughout the twentieth century to the present day, numerous attempts have been made to integrate the arts in the life of the church. Various initiatives were carryover efforts of the latter part of the nineteenth century, such as the educational goals of Chautauqua Institute's summer arts programs. In determining the purposes of art, individuals from a broad range of backgrounds—minister, theologian, philosopher, artist, and layman—have spoken on a host of questions like what is good and bad, why art is made, for whom it is made, what it should look like, how it should sound, just to mention a few. In the process of answering these questions, institutions have been developed, exhibits hung, lectures given, songs created, plays performed, books written, lectures presented—you get the picture. While not exhaustive, this chapter seeks to highlight some of the most significant Creatives and their efforts to shape the renewal.

The Religious Education Association and the Federal Council of Churches

One of the first national events of the new century that helped promote the arts in a broad range of Christian circles occurred in 1903 in Chicago, at the formative meeting of the Religious Education Association. The purpose of the Religious Education Association, as stated in its constitution, was to "promote religious and moral education" across a broad spectrum of disciplines within American culture.[1]

It should be noted that another organization taking shape at this time with direct ties to the goals of the Religious Education Association was the Federal Council of Churches (FCC) of Christ in America. During the 1905 meeting, William H.P. Faunce, President of Brown University, summarized the goals of the FCC in relation to culture:

> "All who follow Him are pursuing His method, and trying to incarnate again the Spirit of Christ, in city and village, in school and college, in home and Church, in business and recreation. They are striving through the slow-moving centuries to make the kingdoms of this world-the kingdoms of literature and science and art-the kingdoms of commerce and industry-the kingdoms of government and education and religion-to make all these the Kingdom of Our Lord and of His Christ."[2]

One of the areas mentioned by Faunce, and intended for influence, was art. J. Cleveland Cady, who will be discussed later, was one of the most prominent architects of his day and in attendance during this time. He played a leading role in the founding meetings of the FCC. Cady was also involved in the initial meetings of the Religious Education Association and a member of its Religious Art and Music Department.

University and Seminary Involvement

The historic assembly of the Religious Education Association included representatives from the most esteemed universities, colleges, and seminaries in America of the time including Union Theological Seminary (New York), McCormick Theological Seminary, Chicago Theological Seminary, Harvard University Divinity School, Hartford Theological Seminary, Yale Divinity School, University of Chicago, Oberlin College, Vanderbilt University, Syracuse University, Ohio State University, Columbia University, Brown University, Northwestern University, Tulane University, the University of Kansas, the

Union Theological Seminary
Courtesy of Library of Congress

University of Mississippi and Cornell University to name a few. Church representatives from almost every denomination and nearly all states were present, as well as representatives from libraries, private schools, the press, and public schools.

Department of Religious Art and Music

Areas of culture selected for analysis were called "departments" and included Sunday Schools, Elementary Public Schools, Secondary Public Schools, Churches and Pastors, Private Schools, Teacher Training, Christian Associations, Young People's Societies, the Home, Libraries, the Press, Correspondence Instruction, Summer Assemblies and Religious Art and Music. Each department was charged to investigate the progress of religious and moral education related to its discipline and give a report at the annual meetings of the Religious Education Association. Of particular interest here is the department of Religious Art and Music.

Prominent members of the first board included Caleb T. Winchester, Professor of Rhetoric and English Literature at Wesleyan College; Harrington

Beard; Waldo S. Pratt, Professor of Music at Hartford Theological Seminary; Henry Turner Bailey, Agent of the Massachusetts Board of Education; Howard Duffield, Pastor of Old First Presbyterian Church in New York; Charles H. Farnsworth, Professor of Music at Columbia University; and Harriet Cecil Magee, Teacher at State Normal School, Oshkosh, Wisconsin.

The members of the first board of the Religious Art and Music department were the leaders of their field at that time. For example, Caleb T. Winchester was a professor at Wesleyan University from 1873 to 1920 and also worked on the committee that revised the *Methodist Hymnal*. An author as well, he wrote *Five Short Courses of Reading, Some Principles of Literary Criticism, The Life of John Wesley*, and *A Group of English Essayists*.[3]

An artist, author, teacher, speaker and leader of visual arts in Wisconsin, Harriet Cecil Magee was an active advocate of the arts for many years. In 1908, Magee gave a symposium presentation titled "Art Education in Normal Schools" at the Third International Conference for the Development of Drawing and Art Teaching, held in London.[4] She wrote *Where to Go and What to See: A Short History of Art* in 1932.[5]

The members of the first board of the Religious Art and Music department were the leaders of their field at that time.

Henry Turner Bailey was an author, artist, and educator who worked as Dean of the Cleveland School of Art in 1917.[6] In 1901, he became editor of *School Arts Magazine*, which is still in publication today. Bailey also played an important role in the Picture Study Movement, which took place at the beginning of the twentieth century and advocated the study of pictures as a means of appreciating art.[7] He also designed the Arts and Crafts Quadrangle at the Chautauqua Institute.[8] His books included *The Great Painters Gospel, Pictures Representing Scenes and Incidents in the Life of Our Lord Jesus Christ, Art Education, Photography and Fine Art*, and many other titles.

Magee and Bailey were among the founding members of the Religious Education Association and among the first lecturers on art at the convention. Both disparaged the indifference of churches to the potential of the arts, at the same time advancing potential solutions to the situation. In her lecture, Magee promoted the idea of church-sponsored clubs and classes for the study of art and music. For Magee, the foundational principle for the use of art in the church and Sunday school was that "art is the gift of God and must be used unto His glory."[9] She also pointed out the growing role of visual art in secular education as a means of appreciating beauty, culture, and history; and that this should be adopted in churches.[10]

Henry Turner Bailey's lecture proposed the educational advantages of integrating "biblical pictures" into the curriculum. Beyond the educational benefits, Bailey saw the dawning of a "new day" of visual arts in the church. In his words, "Protestants are beginning to wonder if their God is not the same now that he was when he found Bezaleel the son of Uri and filled him with the Spirit of God, in wisdom, and in understanding, and in knowledge, and in all manner of workmanship…"[11] Further, Bailey associated the renewed use of art by churches as a means to "fulfill anew the prophecy" of Isaiah 60:13.[12]

Waldo S. Pratt's specialization was music and proposed inclusion of a wide range of arts including visual arts, architecture, hymnody, organ music, the liturgy, poetry, and literature. Pratt also recommended historic studies of the arts, drama, opera, galleries, museums, and concert series as spheres for analysis.[13] As a member of Hartford Theological Seminary, he proposed broader inclusion of arts education in seminaries for the ministers of America's churches.

Ralph Adams Cram
©Corbis

Two of the most important architects of the time, J. Cleveland Cady and Ralph Adams Cram, were members of the Religious Education Association and lectured on the educational and spiritual significance of church architecture. Cady proposed four principles for church buildings: durability, sincerity, dignity, and beauty. A factor in achieving these centered on church decoration and since, according to Cady, Protestant churches lacked mural artists, "pictorial collections" should be used till the advent of trained painters.[14] Along with pictures of the churches history, and photographs of the holy land, Cady recommended the use of "illustrations of sacred events" by artists such as Jalabert, Hunt, Hofman, Zimmerman, and Kellar.[15]

Ralph Adams Cram became a prominent promoter of the ideals of Gothic architecture, with multiple examples of his work at Princeton University, as well as numerous ecclesiastical commissions. As an artist, lecturer, and author, perhaps no other Creative of the period was a stronger advocate for the educational, cultural, and spiritual role of the arts. *The Ministry of Art*, written in 1914, is a compilation of several of Cram's public lectures and speeches, in which he delineates a central thesis that "art has performed, and always can perform, as an agency toward the redemption of human character…"[16]

> "Art has performed, and always can perform, as an agency toward the redemption of human character…"
> —RALPH ADAMS CRAM

In essence, this could be considered a summation of Cram's philosophy on the arts in history, education, church, and culture. One concept made throughout the book is that a "new dawn," "new epoch," and "new day" was arising in the relationship of art and religion. At one point Cram states "[i]t is this conviction…that lies at the base of the great turning of religion to art in these latest days."[17] He went on to say, "To every movement, then, toward to the restoration of diplomatic relations between religion and art, the church must give her earnest support."[18] In one of the most eloquent analogies of the book, Cram compares the arts—sculpture, painting, architecture, poetry, music, drama, and ceremony—to a language, and together they are "Pentecostal tongues through which the Holy Spirit manifests himself to all nations" and communicate ultimate realities.[19]

Dorothy Sayers, who was educated at Somerville College, Oxford, and one of the first women to graduate from the university, was a prolific author who wrote in many areas. She was a contemporary of C.S. Lewis, T.S. Eliot, and Charles William. Her book, *The Mind of the Maker*, was published in 1942, and presents God as an artist and creation His work of art.[20] Other books by Sayers,

Begin Here and *Creed or Chaos* set her apart as a Christian scholar willing to speak out for Christian principles.[21]

Catholic Art and Liturgical Renewal

Cram's contemporary, Maurice Lavanoux, helped establish the Liturgical Arts Society in 1928 and served as secretary until it ceased in 1972. Lavanoux became the Society's chief spokesman, influencing the highest levels of the Catholic Church and its perspectives on art and architecture for nearly 40 years. After serving in WWI, Lavanoux stayed in France to attend the Ecole des Beaux Arts. Upon returning to the United States in 1921, he took a series of jobs until 1925, when he found work with Maginnis & Walsh, one of the country's foremost designers of ecclesiastical architecture.[22] One of the stated goals of the Society was to "promote the study and practice of the arts and crafts relating directly to the worship of the Catholic Church."[23] To disseminate the ideas of the Society, Liturgical Arts began publication in 1931.[24]

The Society was part of the larger Liturgical Renewal Movement, which was taking place within the Catholic Church at the time, and included leading intellectuals, patrons, architects, and artists. Perhaps the most influential Catholic philosopher of the early twentieth century, Jacques Maritain corresponded with Lavanoux and the Society, even acting as liaison with the Vatican.[25] Maritain's book, *Art and Scholasticism*, published in the United States in 1930, influenced Lavanoux's aesthetic philosophy, as well as other Catholics interested in liturgical renewal and art. In his lifetime, Lavanoux received four honorary doctoral degrees, lectured extensively in North America, and traveled to Rome as part of a group that was given an audience with Pope John Paul XXIII in Rome.[26]

Esther Newport, known as Sister Esther Newport, founded the Catholic Art Association in 1937 with the goal of "facilitating dialogue about the use of art in religious practices and also to establish principles to guide the creation of Christian art for church use, in education, and in the home." The Association also published *Catholic Art Quarterly* from 1937 to 1970, *The Catholic Elementary Art Guide*, and sponsored exhibitions and conventions.[27] A colleague of Newport, Ade Bethune, also played a significant role in the Association, as well as the Liturgical Renewal Movement. Bethune was also a writer, and acted as liturgical consultant on 300 church designs during her career. A graduate of the National Academy of Design and Cooper Union, Bethune was a multitalented artist who worked in a variety of media and executed commissions for many clients.[28]

In 1976, Father Virgil Funk established the National Association of Pastoral Musicians, an organization than now has 10,000 members[29] made up of "choir directors, organists, guitarists pianists, instrumentalists of all kinds, priests, cantors, and pastoral liturgists."[30] Prior to this, he had been named executive director of the Liturgical Conference, an interdenominational organization that works to renew the liturgy.[31] The Liturgical Conference was founded in 1940 with several goals related to the liturgical life of the church, and of interest here, the liturgical arts.[32]

National Council of Churches

By mid-century, the arts received an important endorsement among mainline Protestant churches in America when the National Council of Churches of Christ was organized from what had been the Federal Council of Churches.[33] As the National Council of Churches (NCC) was being founded, some divisions from the previous organization were merged or eliminated to create new departments. The Department of Worship and the Arts, a new unit of the NCC, was created to promote "education which deepens understanding of worship and the fine arts and to find aids for the encouragement of worship, both public and private."[34]

> By mid-century, the arts received an important endorsement among mainline protestant churches.

Marvin Halverson, theologian and outspoken advocate for arts integration in the life of the church, became executive director of the department from 1952, and served till 1962. The department utilized a variety of methods to carry out its goal, including performances, exhibitions, lectures, and publications. Prominent leaders in the field of the arts, such as Eero Saarinen, one of the foremost architects of the twentieth century, and Alfred Barr, an art historian and the first director of the Museum of Modern Art in New York, worked with the department's program. Other leaders included theologians Paul Tillich and Stanley Hopper.

As director, Halverson contended for contemporary art forms to be utilized which he felt would communicate to modern culture effectively. He and his associates felt that much of American ecclesiastical art and architecture at that time was cliché and outmoded. In 1961, Halverson created the Society for Arts, Religion, and Contemporary Culture and left the NCC. Among SARCC fellows have been nationally known artists, architects, theologians, playwrights, clergy, dancers, musicians, and novelists.[35] The department underwent a name change to the Department of Church and Culture and was directed by Roger Ortmayer from 1966 to 1974.[36]

Writers: Theology, Aesthetics, and Culture

While Halverson and others worked to integrate the arts within the member churches of the NCC, Evangelical scholars began taking up the issue in the 1970s. Philosopher-theologians like Hans Rookmaaker and Francis Schaeffer found fertile ground for their message among another sector of Christianity–Evangelicals, which had grown rapidly since the 1950s, due in part to the public ministries of evangelists Billy Graham and Oral Roberts. While differing with some of the presuppositions of modern art, Rookmaaker and Schaeffer were equally candid in their condemnation of the Evangelical's apathy to the arts and culture.

Born in the Netherlands in 1922, Rookmaaker was an art historian, critic, author, and lecturer in the Dutch Reformed tradition. Once released from Nazi prison camps after World War II, Rookmaaker attended Amsterdam University and studied art history, graduating with his doctorate in 1959. Rookmaaker traveled and lectured extensively in England and America. His book *Modern Art and the Death of a Culture*, which was published in 1970, was a critique of modern art and its philosophical underpinnings.[37] *Art Needs No Justification* called on Christians to reevaluate preconceived notions of their role in engaging culture through the arts. He was especially influenced by the philosophy of Abraham Kuyper and Herman Dooyeweerd.

Theologian and apologist Francis Schaeffer had widespread international influence among evangelical Christians. Schaeffer graduated from Faith Theological Seminary in 1937 and was the recipient of several honorary doctorate degrees. In 1955, he founded L'Abri Fellowship for the purpose of helping answer questions related to a wide range of cultural issues, such as the arts, politics, or social sciences, all in a study center setting.[38] In the book *Art and the Bible*, Schaffer argued that one of the main purposes of art was to glorify God. Concerning the arts Schaeffer stated:

> But there is another side to the lordship of Christ, and this involves the total culture—including the area of creativity. Again, evangelical or biblical Christianity has been weak at this point. About all we have produced is a very romantic Sunday school art. We do not seem to understand that the arts too are supposed to be under the lordship of Christ.[39]

He went on to argue that Christians should use the arts to the glory of God and that works of art were a form of doxology.[40] Schaeffer's book, along with others he authored, provided a foundational polemic for a generation of Christians interested in the arts and culture, especially those who had been involved in the Jesus Movement.

Nicholas Wolterstorff has been professor of theology and philosophy at Yale and Calvin College, as well as serving in numerous visiting professorships. With an impressive academic portfolio, professional distinctions, and memberships in elite intellectual organizations, Wolerstorff has pioneered research in the interrelation of theology, philosophy, and aesthetics for many years. He gave the Wilde Lectures at Oxford, the Gifford Lectures at St. Andrews University, and the Stone Lectures at Princeton University.[41] Among his many books, *Art in Action: Toward a Christian Aesthetic*, which was written in 1980, offered new perspectives on the arts and encouraged Christians to value the arts in all aspects of life.

Like Wolterstorff, Calvin Seerveld's pioneering work in aesthetics and philosophy were influenced by the work of Abraham Kuyper. Seerveld's first book on the topic, *Rainbows for a Fallen World*, was written in 1980. In this book Seerveld deals with the imagination and with the Christian's role in creating art and influencing culture. Among his other books are *A Christian Critique of Art and Literature* and *Bearing Fresh Olive Leaves*. A graduate of Calvin College, Seerveld also earned a Master's degree from the University of Michigan, and a Doctorate from the Free University of Amsterdam.[42]

Several prominent themes emerged from the 1990s into the twenty-first century, including the biblical basis for various art forms, imagination and creativity, and interpretation of contemporary art forms. Significant contributors to the arts and culture dialogue included Frank Gaebelein and Leland Ryken. The relationship of art and truth and how each should influence Christianity's interaction with culture were the theme of Gaebeleins's book *The Christian, the Arts and the Truth*, published in 1985. Gaebelein, who was a pianist and writer, and coeditor of *Christianity Today*, was headmaster of Stony Brook School, which he founded, for 41 years.[43] Leland Ryken, a prolific award winning author and Emeritus Professor of English, has taught at Wheaton College for over four decades. His book, *The Liberated Imagination*, written in 1989, stressed the role of the imagination and the arts in the life of the church.

In 1991, Gene Veith, wrote *State of the Arts: From Bezalel to Mapplethorpe*, which was an historical–critical overview of the arts in the Western culture, and advanced a biblical view of creativity. Veith, who has authored numerous books, is member of The Alliance of Confessing Evangelicals, Provost, and Professor of Literature at Patrick Henry College, and past Culture Editor for *World Magazine*.[44]

As an author, producer, and educator, Colin Harbinson has played a prominent role for over 40 years in the arts renewal movement as both a leader and pioneer. In 1978 Harbinson wrote the play "Toymaker & Son," while working as headmaster of a school in England. This groundbreaking play has become an international phenomenon, and will be covered further in the chapter on dance. Most recently, Harbinson served as Dean of the Arts at Belhaven College and is the founder and International Director of StoneWorks Global Arts Initiative. Harbinson's book, *The Arts and Cultural Restoration*, gives a biblical perspective on the role artists can play in renewing culture. Harbinson has lectured extensively about arts renewal in America and around the world.[45] One of Rory Noland's major contributions has been to bring an awareness of the spiritual needs of artists and methods to provide for their discipleship. In 1999, he wrote *The Heart of the Artist*, which was intended as a discipleship resource for those working with artists. This was followed in 2004 with *Thriving as an Artist in Church: Hope and Help for You and Your Ministry Team*. Noland served as music director at Willow Creek Community Church for 20 years.[46]

The Arts and Networking

Since the 1990s, Makoto Fujimura has played a significant role in shaping perspectives on the role of Christianity, arts, and culture. He is a prolific artist, speaker, and writer, with numerous exhibits, publications, conferences, and lecture presentations to his credit. In 1992, Fujimura created International Arts Movement (IAM), which is a "community of artists and creative catalysts gathered to wrestle with the deep questions of art, faith, and humanity."[47] This organization hosts global gatherings, conferences, and artistic encounters. In 2011, the Fujimura Institute was established as means for collaboration between artists from different fields.[48] In the same year, Fujimura collaborated with Bruce Herman, Christopher Theofanidis, and Jeremy Begbie to establish the Four Qu4rtets, an exhibition that was inspired by work by T.S. Eliot, and intended to travel around the world. Most recently, Fujimura was named the 2014 Religion and the Arts Award winner by the American Academy of Religion.[49]

Jeremy Begbie, who is Thomas A. Langford Research Professor in Theology in the Duke Divinity School, has lectured worldwide on theology and the arts. Prior to coming to Duke, Begbie had founded the Theology through the Arts Project in 2000 at the University of St. Andrews, which was essentially replicated with the Duke Initiative in Theology and the Arts.[50] As we will see in a later chapter, this also represented a growing trend among seminaries to provide research opportunities in theology and the arts.

Within the first decade of the twenty-first century, Byron Spradlin, who has worked over a quarter century with Artists in Christian Testimony International, was appointed by the Lausanne Movement as Senior Associate for the Arts. In this capacity, Spradlin continues to lead strategic efforts regarding arts renewal in churches and cultures around the world.

Pioneer Creative Catalyst's Story

Dr. Colin Harbinson,
International Director of Stoneworks Global Arts Initiative

A VISION FOR THE NATIONS

The photograph of a defiant Boris Yeltsin, standing on top of a tank outside the Russian White House in August 1991, signaled a turning point in history. Less than two years after the Berlin Wall had crumbled, this newly elected Russian president courageously stared down the Communist hardliners who were attempting a coup in Moscow. The unthinkable happened; the communists were defeated, the Cold War ended, and the world pulled back from the threat of nuclear war.

Just prior to this historic moment, a member of the St. Petersburg city government had given me an official invitation to bring artists from around the world to participate in an historic East-West cultural exchange festival. That invitation to "bring the hope and spiritual encouragement we need" was re-affirmed immediately following the attempted coup. At that time I was asked to help "rehabilitate" the image of a palace that had been a symbol of communist oppression for over 70 years. Accompanied by members of the new government, I entered the Belezorsky Palace on Nevsky Prospeckt. It had remained sealed since the communist leaders had been evicted a few weeks earlier. As the seals were removed from the doors of the building that was to become my headquarters for the next three months, I had a profound sense that God was going to open the doors of nations closed to His truth, and that He was going to do it through the arts.

As 1991 ended and a new year was born, 365 artists, business people, and spiritual leaders from more than 30 countries participated in Sacred Fire, the first East-West cultural exchange festival. Music, dance, theatre and visual arts encounters were held in venues across the city of St. Petersburg in collaboration with hundreds of Russian artists. I watched the language of the arts dismantle religious, political and cultural barriers, replacing them with bridges of understanding, relationship, and hope.

My engagement with the arts had an improbable beginning. I was born in London, England, the year after WWII ended. My conservative Christian upbringing insulated me from the arts. Learning to play the piano was the only concession to this sphere of human activity that was otherwise deemed "worldly." While entering my first movie theatre at 19 years of age, all I could think about was "what would happen if Jesus came back and caught me watching a movie?" I had often heard those disconcerting words.

It was during my initial year at college that I first became aware that God had given me creative gifts. It was 1965, and cultural change was in the air. The Beatles were topping the charts and Christian rock music in Europe was in its infancy. A fellow student and founder of one of these rock bands asked if I had ever played the drums. His drummer was sick and the band had an important upcoming gig. Even after I responded with a definitive "no" to his question, he still persisted. I reluctantly agreed to give it a try. We rehearsed together for a few days, and that weekend I found myself playing in my first gospel rock concert. I went on to play with the band for several years.

Growing up, I never had a real opportunity to explore my creative gifts. Now I felt a palpable excitement as I began to express what God had placed within me. This new journey I found myself on quickly hit a barrier when my studies required movement classes. When the dance professor asked the class to pretend we were flowers and to open and close our petals in time with the music, it was almost too much for me to handle. Yet, as I persisted, I discovered a newfound freedom of expression and love for dance that has never left me. I pursued postgraduate study in the arts and created and choreographed dance-theatre productions for my students in the public school system. By now the arts were my passion, and they had also become central to my teaching methodology. As time passed, I continued to love what I was doing, but knew a transition was coming, although I did not know the timing or the nature of the change.

As a young boy, I had been deeply impacted by the dramatic events that unfolded in the Amazon Jungle, when five young American missionaries were speared to death by a ruthless Stone Age tribe. Shortly after, at the age of 12, I had a powerful and life-changing encounter with Christ. In my late teens I found myself strongly drawn to foreign missions. But in my twenties I settled down, got married, had a family and was enjoying a successful career in education. By the late 70s, I had formed a dance company that began work on Dayuma—a new production I had written and choreographed, based on this tribal story that had moved me so much.

I began to dream of having a full-time company of gifted dancers like the ones I was working with, who would live, work, and travel together to perform works that would glorify God and impact people's lives. Although I did not know it then, my dream was to prove too small.

Around this time, I received word that my dance company had been invited to perform at the Edinburgh Festival—Europe's most prestigious arts festival. I was thrilled beyond measure. The dream was becoming a reality. I envisioned this as the launching pad that would propel me into a new sphere of artistic involvement and excellence; but God had other plans.

It was during a run of Dayuma at a theatre in Birmingham, England, that He got my attention one morning. The call to foreign missions that I had been drawn to years earlier was now ringing loudly in my ear. Instead of elation, I found myself resistant. I told my wife that I thought God was asking me to give up my teaching career by the end of the year to enable our family to join Youth With a Mission—a mission organization that we had become acquainted with in recent years. My hopes of her sharing my disenchantment with this absurd notion quickly dissipated when she told me she had known for some time that this was the direction God was leading us in.

Now I was totally confused. To my thinking, this was not good timing. In the personal struggle that ensued, I came to the point where, if I was going to take this radical step, I had to write my letter of resignation. I just couldn't make myself do it. The 14 years of my life that I had already invested would be wasted. God had clearly led me into teaching and, on top of that, the Edinburgh Festival was closing in. Now I was to throw it all away and join a mission organization?

I went for a walk in a wooded area close to my home to be alone with the Lord. I told Him that I wanted to do His will, but that I needed to hear His voice and know that this was really what He wanted me to do. As I decided to sit down on a nearby log and meditate on Scripture, my Bible fell open at Hebrews 10. I began to read that Jesus came to "do the will of His Father." That was my desire, and I was encouraged. But it was the next few words that gripped my heart: "He takes away the first, to establish the second." Tears of joy began to flow down my cheeks. I knew exactly what God was saying to me. He had called me into teaching, but now He had something new for me to do. I went home, wrote my letter of resignation, and a few months later my family and I were in Youth With a Mission. I was tasked to develop the arts in the context of this global mission organization.

To work fulltime in YWAM, as it was called, you had to go through a Discipleship Training School (DTS). I suspected I didn't need one—I was already a leader in my church and had preached around the country—but it was a non-negotiable requirement. This program changed my life. I can only describe what happened to me as "spiritual open heart surgery." I soon began to realize that there was much in my life that was not pleasing to God. I wept, this time in sorrow. He showed me the pride and arrogance that had so captivated my heart, and the competitive attitude I had toward other Christians involved in the arts. There was so much of "self" mixed in with my desire to serve God. I thought he had closed the door on my dream. Now I saw that he had lovingly prevented me from entering more fully into the world of the arts at that time. I would have been seduced by success and destroyed by failure.

Recognizing the need for godly character in my walk with the Lord, along with my earlier experience of needing a place to discover, nurture and develop my own God-given creativity, have been motivational factors in my work with artists and emerging artists over the years. To enable them to find their artistic voice without ensuring that they have the opportunity to develop godly character in their lives is like sending sheep to the slaughter. I have sadly observed the lives of excellent artists whose call to serve God was hijacked by an unrighteous lifestyle or ungodly choices.

The second part of my discipleship school was a practicum in Venice, Italy, where what we had been taught was put into action, alongside hundreds of other students from across Europe. On my arrival, I was asked if I would recruit gifted dancers and actors in the program and mount the dance-theatre production I had just written for the children at my school. Toymaker & Son was an allegory of the gospel. God was the Toymaker. Jesus was the Toymaker's son who becomes a toy and goes to live in a rebellious Toyland, in order to restore the broken relationship between the toys and the Toymaker. The publicity described it as "the epic account of the most powerful rebellion in history, the greatest love story in the universe, and the most daring rescue plan ever conceived."

Following the premier performance in Venice for the other mission students, there was hardly a dry eye. Audience members began to describe how the story of God's love had become more real, how they had gained new spiritual insight through watching Toymaker & Son. I was taken back by the response. When we performed in St. Marco Square, I watched the large crowd that gathered alternate between tears and laughter. Little did I know that this production would later be performed before world leaders and whole governments; from Royal Command Performances to the official program of Olympic Games and World Cup soccer events; in village squares and prestigious theatres in over 70 countries. God was showing me that His vision was so much bigger than mine.

Most of my years with Youth With Mission were based in Canada, where we arrived from England with five suitcases and five dollars, in 1979. It was there that my dream to develop an arts training program with a discipleship component became a reality. For years, Christians from around the world came to be trained at the School of Creative Ministry in Cambridge, Ontario. At the height of its success, I had 95 full-time faculty dedicated to the vision. These were heady years of seeing my vision for the arts flourish.

However, the seemingly assured sale of our 43-acre facility fell through, after we had already gone ahead and purchased another location. We had planned to build a new, purpose-built arts training complex, but had made a fundamental business mistake. Now we were caught in the middle. We prayed long and hard that God would redeem the situation, but in the end, the bank took both properties. What do you do when your vision crumbles?

It was a dark time for me. I began to think that maybe God was not really interested in the arts after all. What about all the other times I believed I heard His voice and had stepped out in faith. Had I imagined that? I asked Him to let me know if He had allowed it for a greater purpose, to just whisper in my ear and let me know His presence. The extended silence was profound. Everything that could be shaken within me was shaken. To this day I do not fully understand why God permitted it to happen, why He didn't answer our prayers. Yet, through his grace, I was ultimately able to move on and not allow this failure to birth doubt and cynicism in my heart. I still love and trust Him with all my heart, yet like Jacob, who wrestled with the Lord, I also walk with a "limp."

I continued on with my responsibilities with YWAM for several years as International Dean of the College of the Arts at the University of the Nations. As the decade came to a close, so did our 21 years of service with the mission. My own arts organization, International Festival of the Arts, had just completed what the Chinese government described as the largest international festival of its kind in the history of the nation.

I had taken 300 artists from 20 countries as an official part of the 1999 World Exposition that was held in Kunming, China. This was the most thrilling of all of our cultural exchanges, with over 400 Chinese artists involved. One highlight of the festival was the first opportunity in at least seven decades for a Chinese audience to hear the full score of Handel's Messiah—performed collaboratively by Chinese and international artists, along with accompanying Chinese subtitles. The next day, a headline in the newspaper that went out to over 40 million people in this communist nation declared, "Messiah Touches Hearts." That summed up the hopes and prayers of these artists of faith that God would reveal Himself through the building of authentic relationships with Chinese artists, as well as through artistic works lovingly offered to Chinese audiences.

Soon after returning home from China, I was offered the position of Dean of the Arts at Belhaven University—formerly Belhaven College—in the capital city of Jackson, Mississippi. During my years as the dean, God graciously allowed me another opportunity to build a quality arts program, this time at a Christian university. Today, with its new custom designed facilities and gifted arts faculty, it is one of only 30 universities and colleges in the United States to be nationally accredited in dance, theatre, music and the visual arts.

Back in the early days of my work in the arts, the Lord spoke to me through Isaiah 62:10, "Pass through, pass through the gates! Prepare the way for the people. Build up, build up the highway! Remove the stones. Raise a banner for the nations." (NIV)

Reading that Scripture, I understood the Lord to say to me that I would not live to see the fulfillment of the vision he had placed in my heart. His calling on my life was to help be a highway-builder and a stone-remover, so that future generations would be able to go further than this generation without stumbling on stones that were in their path. There are still many "stones" in the church, and in the life of the artist, that must be identified and removed before we can fully enter into all that God has prepared for us as artists and culture-shapers.

As I look back on the past 40 to 50 years, I see that as Christians we have made huge strides in understanding the place of the arts in the life and mission of the Church, and its individual members. Yet we still have a long way to go. What encourages me the most is that we are all part of the same ongoing story. Along with my peers in the arts, I was able to stand on the shoulders of people like Francis Schaeffer and Hans Rookmaaker. They prepared the way for so many believers by removing some of the "stones" of misunderstanding that were preventing us from engaging our culture and embracing our role as culture makers.

To the extent that we are faithful, the next generation of emerging artists will stand on our shoulders. They will not have to fight the same battles. Understanding that we all play a part in the same unfolding story of God's redemptive purposes throughout the generations gives me a wonderful perspective on my life and work. I could not have participated meaningfully without those who went before and those who will now follow. They bracket my life and work, giving it context and meaning. In this light, even my failures can be embraced as the seedbed of someone else's success. In Christ we participate in the same story, with the same purpose, and for the same ultimate conclusion—the restoration of all things to God's full creational intention.

We are again standing in an historic moment. The arts today are shaping global culture in unprecedented ways. God is calling and preparing artists and emerging artists of faith to connect their creative gifts with His redemptive purposes. They were born for such a time as this. Those who have gone before and now comprise that great "cloud of witnesses" will be cheering them on. I for one will rejoice as they dream bigger dreams and receive greater support than did my generation—as God continues to restore the arts back to His people and open the doors of nations closed to His truth.

www.stoneworks-arts.org

Pioneer Creative Catalyst's Story

Jeremie Begbie,
Thomas A. Langford Research Professor in Theology, Duke Divinity School; Senior Member at Wolfson College, Cambridge University

Jeremy S. Begbie is the inaugural Thomas A. Langford Research Professor in Theology at Duke Divinity School, North Carolina. He teaches systematic theology, and specializes in the interface between theology and the arts. He is also Senior Member at Wolfson College, Cambridge, and an Affiliated Lecturer in the Faculty of Music at the University of Cambridge.

Educated in Scotland and at Cambridge, he began professional life as a pastor before going to teach theology at Ridley Hall, Cambridge. Since 2009 he has been teaching at Duke University, while spending much of the year in Cambridge, developing links between the two universities. At Duke he has founded *Duke Initiatives in Theology and the Arts* (http://divinity.duke.edu/initiatives-centers/dita)

Begbie's particular research interest is the interplay between music and theology. He is concerned to show how the resources of the Christian intellectual tradition bear on the theory and practice of music, believing that these riches are woefully underexplored by both Christians and non-Christians. At the same time, he believes that music has unique powers to help Christians think through their faith, unlocking the truth of Scripture in ways that have momentous consequences. Moreover, he believes what is true of music here is true of all the arts.

He is author of a number of books, including *Voicing Creation's Praise: Towards a Theology of the Arts* (T&T Clark); *Theology, Music and Time* (CUP); *Resounding Truth: Christian Wisdom in the World of Music* (Baker/SPCK); and *Music, Modernity, and God* (OUP). He is a professionally trained and active musician, and has taught widely in many parts of the world, including the US and UK, Australia, Israel, Hong Kong and South Africa.

THREE

Theatre

"It is coming to be generally recognized that the first practical step toward the church becoming the center of the art life of a Christian people, is in the proper use of drama as an art form for religious service."
—MARTHA CANDLER, 1922, In *Drama In Religious Service*

Vaudeville Show.
Courtesy of Library of Congress

The American pageantry movement, which peaked from 1900 to 1925, featured dramatic reenactments of local, regional, and national history.[1] Often staged outdoors, communities across the country would be involved in the production of these events. While playing a critical role in the social reform movement of the time, it would also influence the church for years to come. Although the educational use of drama had slowly grown during the first decade of the twentieth century, by the end of World War I, churches, denominations, and other religious organizations came to realize the potential for drama.

"The Wayfarer," written in 1919 by Reverend James E. Crowther for the Centenary celebration of Methodist missions held in Columbus, Ohio, advanced the drama movement significantly across denominations. For years, Methodist churches had banned theater attendance by its members. However, a notable endorsement of drama is evidenced in the letter sent by the Methodist church to the press about this production. It states, "[t]he church is beginning to learn that there is a tremendous potential force in the dramatic presentation of religious themes, and it purposes that men shall *see* as well as *hear* them."[2]

In 1922, Martha Candler, author of Drama in Religious Service stated, "Not long ago, the linking of the words 'Christianity' and 'the stage' would have offended Christian ears." [3] According to Candler, drama was being used for more than spontaneous missionary plays, Sunday school lessons, and social group entertainment and was being adapted for expressive purposes, in the "acted sermon, in ritual, liturgy and church holiday services."[4] Writing in 1924, Madeleine Sweeney Miller said confidently, that pageantry "has been reclaimed and harnessed to higher aims enriched with spiritual content…"[5]

The American pageantry movement peaked from 1900 to 1925.
Courtesy of Library of Congress

Denominations and Drama

Denominations and agencies responded by providing resources for churches interested in utilizing the rediscovered medium. These included the Epworth League of the Methodist Episcopal Church (Chicago); the Woman's Foreign Missionary Society of the Methodist Episcopal Church (New York or Boston); the Department of Missionary Education of the Baptist Board of Education, New York; the Pageants and Exhibits Division of the Methodist Episcopal Church; the Department of Missions of Protestant Episcopal Church; the Presbyterian Board of Publication, New York; the Woman's Boards of Foreign and Home Missions of the Presbyterian Church, New York; the Missionary Education Movement, New York; the Religious Drama Committee of the Drama League of America, located in Chicago; and the Religious Drama Committee of the Federal Council of Churches of Christ in America.[6]

In 1923 the Episcopal Actors Guild was created as an offshoot of the Actors Church Alliance, which had its origin in 1899. The founder of ACA, Walter

The Little Church Around the Corner, New York
Courtesy of Library of Congress

Bentley, had turned from acting to become a priest, and actively encouraged the members to form the guild in 1923. The rector of the Church of the Transfiguration (also known as The Little Church Around the Corner), the Reverend Randolph Ray, invited the group to make this church their permanent home. Some of the most famous and influential personalities of the stage have been members of the guild, which continues to the present day.[7]

The Federal Council of Churches

By 1924, the Federal Council of Churches Committee on Religious Drama published *Religious Dramas*, a book listing dramas selected for use in churches. It is significant to note that the Federal Council of Churches around this time was comprised of 30 denominations, nearly 18 million members, 103,113 ministers and approximately 139,000 congregations.[8] The creation of this committee and the production of the book symbolized a major endorsement of drama for a significant portion of the church in that time. In short order, numerous writers created dramas that could be purchased through publishing companies including Pilgrim Press, MacMillan, Abingdon Press, Morehouse Publishing Company, Harper Brothers, and others.

This represented a growing pattern for drama Creatives—both writers and actors—a context for artistic expression. Alice Corbin Henderson, James S. Stevens, Kate Douglas Wiggins, Mary E. Telford, H. Augustine Smith, Reverend C.L. Bates, C.H. Jarrett, A.M. Buckton, Percy Mackaye, Katherine Lord, and Florence Converse were just a few writers mentioned by Martha Candler in *Drama in Religious Service*.[9] Titles included *Bible Plays, Shorter Bible Plays, Bible Study through Educational Drama, Abraham and Isaac, Friends of Jesus, Biblical Dramas, The Resurrection of Our Lord, Star of the East, Rebekah, The Rich Young Man*, and many others. Plays were also available for Christmas, Easter, the Fourth of July, and Thanksgiving.[10]

Drama and Higher Education

Drama was also included in higher education when, in 1918, the Department of Fine Arts in Religious Education was established at Boston University, a Methodist institution located in Massachusetts. H. Augustine Smith, who served as its first chairman, was an author, director, and speaker, whose work would influence Creatives for years to come. Smith wrote several books including *Worship in the Church School through Music, Pageantry and Pictures, The Organization and Administration of Choirs, Lyric Religion*, and others. For one observer at the time, the creation of the department confirmed the belief that "the church must again become the mother of artists and the generous patron of the arts." The program offered course work in areas such as music, poetry, art, and drama. Among the goals of the department was to educate leaders who would serve as "directors of religious education in local parishes; directors and instructors in the week-day schools of religious education which are being widely organized; religious directors for communities; religious directors for settlements and Christian associations; educational superintendents for denominational boards; home and foreign missions educators and executives; special directors for community institutes of religious education, conventions, and schools of method in religious teaching."[11]

By 1948, the University of Chicago Divinity School created a program in religion and the arts, led by Preston Roberts.[12] In 1956, Union Theological Seminary, located in New York City, established a program in Religious Drama which eventually became the Department of Speech, Drama, and Communication, under the leadership of Robert Seaver.[13] Around the same time, Harvard Divinity School established a similar program. The purpose of these programs was to educate future teachers and pastors about the role of the arts in "understanding and interpreting" their faith.[14]

National Council of Churches

On the national level, the Federal Council of Churches, which was founded in 1908, merged with other organizations in 1950 to become the National Council of Churches of Christ in the USA. As mentioned in an earlier chapter, the Department of Worship and the Arts, a new unit of the NCC, was created to promote "education which deepens understanding of worship and the fine arts and to find aids for the encouragement of worship, both public and private."

At the same time, denominational organizations took shape that included drama, as well as the other arts. In 1955, a group of Methodist musicians met in Colorado to formulate a national fellowship of Methodist church musicians. Over a period of more than 50 years, the organization, known as the "Fellowship," has grown to include drama, art, dance, and contemporary worship. The Fellowship hosts conferences, training events, competitions, and publishes *Worship Arts* journal.[15]

> **At the same time, denominational organizations took shape that included drama, as well as the other arts.**

While many churches and denominational colleges continued to feature traditional forms of drama during the 60s and 70s, major cultural changes opened new venues for Jesus movement Creatives. Street theater, skits, and drama troupes were just a few art forms used to communicate their message. The Holy Ghost Players, for example, toured regularly with the Resurrection Band.[16] The Jesus Movement took place in a cultural milieu which included musical dramas such as *Hair*, *Jesus Christ Superstar*, and *Godspell*. Ralph Carmichael, who had years of experience in the entertainment industry, saw the need to create drama that spoke to

Christian youth in musical language. Carmichael, who founded Light Records, was uniquely positioned to provide the impetus needed for such endeavors. Working with Kurt Kaiser, of Word, and Billy Ray Hearn, the Christian musicals *Good News, Tell It Like It Is*, and *Natural High* were created. At the same time, para-church drama organizations began to form in the 60s, offering new opportunities for creative expression and ministry.

Covenant Players

California based Covenant Players was founded in 1963 by Charles Tanner, a prolific playwright, who wrote over 3,500 plays in his lifetime. After serving in WW II, Tanner worked in Hollywood in the film industry. By 1981, Covenant Players had traveled extensively in North America, as well as internationally to Europe, Australia, Latin America, the Far East and Africa. The doctrinal statement of the organization declares:

> "Covenant Players exists to communicate the Lord Jesus Christ through the medium of drama..."
>
> —COVENANT PLAYERS, FOUNDED BY CHARLES TANNER

> "Covenant Players exists to communicate the Lord Jesus Christ through the medium of drama. Our head is Christ, the Son of the only God, Lord of our lives; acceptance of Him is the only means of salvation."[17]

In 1987, Tanner received an Angel Award from Religion in Media. Since his death in 2006, Covenant Players continues to carry on the vision of its founder. Most recently, the group has worked as Artist Associates with World Vision and continues outreach in various parts of the world.[18]

A.D. Players

At about the same time, the A.D. Players, based in Houston, Texas, was founded in 1967 by Jeanette Clift George, an accomplished author, speaker, and playwright. A.D. Players, according to its mission statement, was established as "a professional theater ministry communicating through various mediums under the creative signature of God."[19] By 1975, the Players created a touring company, and in the same year George starred in "The Hiding Place", and was nominated for a Golden Globe Award. A.D. Players has performed in churches, conferences, and on college campuses. By 1983, the Players were performing internationally with trips to the Bahamas and Europe. In 1990, the Theater Arts Academy was created, and by 1992 the first year round children's theater was formed. Today A.D. Players continues to offer a number of dramas for all ages.[20]

Lamb's Players

Lamb's Players, a Street Theatre troupe, was founded in 1971 by Steve Terrell, who taught drama at Minnesota based Bethel College, and Glen Hansen, one of Terrell's students. By 1972, the company moved to San Diego, California, and began national outreach efforts in colleges, prisons, churches, and Renaissance Fairs using art forms like mime and puppetry troupes, a dance company, and juggling and magic acts. Since 1994, the company has added performance space in two buildings and has an annual audience of over 100,000.[21]

Sight & Sound Theatre

In 1976, Glen Eshelman founded Pennsylvania based Sight & Sound Theatre, reported to be the "largest faith-based live theatre in the country."[22] Eshelman showed interest in art early on, painting and photographing landscapes at his family farm. Over time, these were presented in churches, schools, and civic organizations across the country. From this idea grew the Sight and Sound Theatres, located in Pennsylvania and Missouri. The mission of the organization is to "present the Gospel of Jesus Christ and sow the Word of God into the lives of our customers, guests and fellow workers by visualizing and dramatizing the scriptures, through inspirational productions, encouraging others and seeking always to be dedicated and wise stewards of our God-given talents and resources."[23] By 2012, the organization's facilities featured two state-of-the-art 2,000 seat theaters and an array of Biblically based dramas, with nearly a million visitors in attendance in that year alone.[24]

Acacia Theatre

Wisconsin based Acacia Theatre Company was formed in 1980 as a touring company and is the lone professional Christian theater company in the state. Acacia's programs are meant to reach a wide audience, both Christian and non-Christian alike. The company began with a "desire to integrate art and faith by presenting theatre that would express the experiences and positive moral values important to members of the Christian faith."[25] In 1983, the company added main stage productions and has used a variety of venues including churches, theaters, and most recently the Concordia University's Todd Wehr Auditorium. Four plays are produced each season as well as a Christmas drama. According to the company website, "[m]any works in the company's diverse repertoire are secular, chosen for their ability to spark discussion of Judeo-Christian values and provoke thought about the ramifications an individual's actions can have on those around them and society as a whole."[26] Works such as Thorton Wilder's *Our Town*, William Shakespeare's *A Midsummer Night's Dream*, and Alfred Uhry's *Driving Miss Daisy*, are performed.[27]

Christian Youth Theater

While the afore mentioned organizations offer training for youth and adults, California based Christian Youth Theater began by providing educational opportunities specifically to youth between the ages of 4 and 18. Founded in 1981 as a community theater by Paul and Sheryl Russell, initial meetings literally took place in the family garage. After a successful first season under the name Christian Community Theater, the Russell's were encouraged by parents to offer an after-school theater program. What began with 24 students expanded rapidly and now has annual participation of 4,000 in California alone, with more than 10,000 students in 13 states. Today, Christian Youth Theater is the largest theater of its type in America, offering education through classes, camps, shows, and programs.[28]

The Bride

In 1984 *The Bride* was written by Dony and Reba Rambo McGuire with Gary Thurman and J. Mark Taylor. MetroChurch in Edmond, Oklahoma, employed Taylor to work as their worship leader and Minister of Creative Arts. Taylor, a multitalented Creative immediately went to work producing the theatrical version of "The Bride" for the 1987 Easter season. The production was a huge success, with thousands of people from at least 22 states and other nations attending over its several year history of production. It was distributed on video throughout the United States and in several countries, as well as airing worldwide on the Trinity Broadcasting Network. In 1997 and 1998, it was performed in the Mabee Center at Oral Roberts University.

In 1988, the MetroSchool of Fine Arts was founded by Taylor to train students to glorify and honor God through their gifts. Taylor envisioned an arts school in which professional musicians, dancers, actors, and other artists who were part of the ministries of MetroChurch could share their gifts with young students in the church – raising up an "army of artists" to bring glory to God. In 2001, MetroSchool of the Arts merged with Victory School of Fine Arts. In 2000, Taylor was invited to join the Board of Directors of Oklahoma Alliance for Liturgy and the Arts, a multidenominational-Evangelical group of artists. Outreach efforts of the group have included seminars, historic church tours, sacred art shows, and conferences, all with the goal of enriching the churches of Oklahoma through arts integration.[29]

While it would be impossible to list the numerous drama organizations formed since mid-century, other groups would include Taproot Theatre (1976), Team Ministries Contemporary Christian Drama (1976), Saltworks Theater (1981), and Trinity House Theater (1981).

Christians in the Theatre Arts

By the late 80s, Christians in the Theatre Arts was established with the goal of providing a national network for theatre artists. Since its inception, the group has developed a number of artistic initiatives including scholarly grants, festivals, publications, and workshops, as well as regional, national, and international conferences. National events hosted by CITA in 2013 include the Latin American Conference, held in San Juan, Puerto Rico. Secondary School Theatre Festivals, meant to provide opportunities for high school students in public, private, and home school environments, are also a feature of the organization. Solo, duo, and ensemble musical theater were featured, as well as events for contrasting and Shakespeare monologues.[30]

Willow Creek Church, founded in 1975, also began using theater as a means of reaching "seekers" who were interested in church but not ready to commit to its traditional forms. Willow Creek would go on to model the use of the arts in a local church reaching the culture into the twenty-first century. Among these are the United Methodist Church, Southern Baptist, American Baptist, Wesleyan, Lutheran, Assemblies of God, Church of God in Christ, Presbyterian, and Catholic, to name a few. Two examples would include the productions the *Night of Miracles* and *Virginia Christmas Spectacular*.

The Night of Miracles: A Journey to Bethlehem

In 2007 an outreach was born through the Worship and Fine Arts Ministry of the Buena Vista Pentecostal Holiness Church, in Buena Vista, Virginia, that is known as *Night of Miracles: A Journey to Bethlehem*. The town of Bethlehem was recreated with the help of area churches and donated supplies. A nightly crew and cast of almost 100 volunteers from the church and community re-enact the Christmas story through "a live, interactive, walk-through presentation of the nativity." The re-enactment is about 20 minutes in length. Highlights include the appearance of the three kings as they follow the star, Joseph and Mary traveling near Bethlehem, the angels' appearance to the shepherds, and the presentation of the gifts from the Magi. The outreach's mission states, "it provides a creative vehicle that carries the salvation message to thousands who would never otherwise enter the doors of a local church."[31]

Virginia Christmas Spectacular

Thomas Road Baptist Church, located in Lynchburg, Virginia, presents a Broadway-style production called the *"Virginia Christmas Spectacular"* each holiday season. 500,000 lights, and a cast and crew of more than 350 members are utilized. A live orchestra performs an original musical score. Acting, singing, dancing, costuming, multimedia, props, and stage designs are all aspects of the production. Originally titled the *"Living Christmas Tree"*, the show has been a tradition for over 40 years, drawing crowds in the tens of thousands.[32]

Today, churches across a wide array of denominations include drama as part of their ministry outreach. These have taken various forms including dinner theater, skits, full performances, one act plays, outdoor performances, seasonal plays, sermon illustrations, and workshops. A variety of skills are needed in this type of ministry and include acting, script writing, technology, directing, set design, costume design, makeup, and sound."

Pioneer Creative Catalyst's Story

Chuck Neighbors,
Founder and Director, Master's Image Productions

Chuck Neighbors is the founder and director of Master's Image Productions, a ministry through the theatrical arts since 1984. Chuck and artist associates of MIP primarily perform solo theater pieces in churches, universities, conferences and other organizations. In addition to performing, they also conduct workshops on drama, storytelling and communication.

Chuck discovered his love for the theater as a child performing in church and school productions. Raised in the church and becoming a follower of Christ at a young age, Chuck also felt the call to ministry as a teenager. It wasn't until attending Carson Newman College in Jefferson City, TN that he began to see how that calling would be worked out, as he pursued studies in theater and religion. Between semesters he was cast as assistant to the director and understudy to all male roles in the Smoky Mountain Passion Play. In the course of one summer, he would play every male role in the production—Judas one night and Jesus the next. It was here that he began to learn about the possibilities for using the arts and theater to communicate the Gospel of Jesus.

Chuck left college in 1975 to join Covenant Players, an international touring theater company based in Southern California. It was here that Chuck was able to combine his love for theater with his calling to ministry. He toured with the Players for nine and a half years, hundreds of roles in thousands of performances across the United States and Canada, as well as Japan and Korea. Here he also met his wife, Lorie and together they traveled and performed as leaders and directors for Covenant Players. They managed offices for the company in Ohio and Oregon, as well as worked in the ministry headquarters in California.

In 1984, while living in Portland, OR Chuck left Covenant Players to form Master's Image Productions. He wrote directed and performed a one-man show adapted from Charles Sheldon's Christian classic, *In His Steps*. Shortly after he began touring the production in the Pacific Northwest, the presentation caught the attention of David Mains and his nationally syndicated radio program Chapel of the Air. Chuck performed the drama at some events in partnership with Chapel of the Air that brought the ministry into national focus, resulting in numerous invitations to perform across the US and Canada. Chuck has added several other productions to his repertory over the years, but *In His Steps* is still the mainstay and most performed of all the productions of the ministry.

Chuck has taken his ministry to 17 different countries around the world and performed in a variety of settings, including churches, theaters, gymnasiums, airplane hangars and even on board a submarine. He has traveled by planes, trains and automobiles and even by helicopter to mountaintops in Korea performing for US military troops. In addition to productions on Christian themes he performed and toured a production called Scenes Unseen to schools and colleges that dealt with the subject of drug and alcohol abuse.

In addition to traveling and performing, Chuck has written numerous books of script collections for both Baker Books and Lillenas Publishing. He is the author of several articles on the arts and worship. He has been a conference speaker and has conducted workshops for groups large and small on the use of the arts in ministry. His book *Drama Now!*, a training resource for drama ministry, resulted in a 3-year national tour of drama workshops, which helped to establish drama ministries in numerous churches across the country.

Chuck put much of his theory to work at Salem Alliance Church in Salem, Oregon where he served as Artist in Residence for five years. Here he established an ongoing drama ministry that also grew to include an improvisational theater group. That group not only performed at the church, but also did a weekly community performance as well as corporate performances and bookings at venues outside the church. As other artists of faith took notice of Chuck's work, some would seek his assistance. Chuck began mentoring artists and some of these artists eventually became associates of Master's Image, performing their own productions as a part of the ministry.

From 2001-2014 Chuck began a partnership with World Vision, a Christian relief and development organization. Through this partnership Chuck added a new element to his performances by inviting people to get involved in child sponsorship to help end poverty in third world countries. This has resulted in nearly 6,000 children sponsored through the ministry of Master's Image Productions. In 2014 he began working with Food for the Hungry to help in their efforts. This as extremely significant in proving that the arts can have an impact not only on a local audience but indeed effect change around the globe.

Chuck continues his work based in Salem, Oregon along with his wife Lorie. He has three children and as of this writing one grandchild on the way!

FOUR

Music

"What is important is the fact that music must communicate the gospel.
God has never promised to bless any particular musical form,
only to bless His Word."

—RALPH CARMICHAEL,
GOSPEL MUSIC HALL OF FAME INDUCTEE INFORMATION

Music for the Nation:
American Sheet Music:
Approved in Christ
Courtesy of Library of Congress

While some of the arts took decades to find expression in twentieth century Christianity, pioneering musical Creatives appropriated the religious fervor of the nineteenth century to influence the coming century with new talent, musical forms, and industries. As mentioned earlier, the shape note system, singing schools, songwriters, and camp meeting revivals were among the many factors shaping musical taste and expression at the beginning of the twentieth century.

Shape Notes and Singing Schools

Dating back to early eighteenth century New England, singing schools were meant to reform church music, worship services, and educate churchgoers. Shape notes were developed in the South to improve the ability of Southern

A group of singers from Quemado who are competing for the Catron County championship at the Pie Town, New Mexico, singing convention
Courtesy of Library of Congress

populations to read and sing together. The most popular method for training was through the singing schools. While education in the South lagged behind, Northern students received music education in the growing public school system. Shape note schools would come a century later and would remain even after those in the North diminished.[1]

Teachers would set up local 10-day schools that provided music education and were tailored to meet the artistic needs of the interested individuals from the community by providing flexible times for learning. The fundamentals of the shape note music system were taught, as well as music theory, leading, and sight-reading, with a culminating public performance.[2] Schools were held in various states such as Mississippi, Alabama, Texas, South Carolina, Georgia, Arkansas, and North Carolina.[3] Once students had enough knowledge of the system, they could then offer lessons of their own.

Students who exhibited artistic promise and could afford the cost would attend normal schools, which lasted 4 weeks and offered exposure to a variety of well-known teachers and their musical specializations. Normal schools prepared future traveling teachers who would represent the publisher's music products, such as songbooks and pamphlets, throughout the communities of the nation. These included older recognized hymns as well as newer gospel songs. The Virginia Normal Music School, later named the Shenandoah Normal Music School in 1880, was one of the first "normals" in the South and was created in 1874 by Aldine Kieffer, one of the partners in the Ruebush-Kieffer Publishing Company.[4]

James David Vaughan and Southern Gospel Music

Born in 1864 in Tennessee, James Vaughan played a founding role in the development of Southern gospel music in the United States. Vaughan's music career was shaped early on by two singing school teachers associated with the Ruebush-Kieffer Music Company, James Berry, and Ephraim Hildebrand. The latter was partner in Roanoke, Virginia-based Hildebrand-Burnett Music Company. While in Texas, Vaughan wrote music, and attended classes in a traveling normal school taught by Hildebrand, and eventually established his own school, the Vaughan Normal School of Music in 1911. He also recruited the well-known music teacher Benjamin C. Unseld, who had taught at Fisk University and worked with the Fisk Jubilee Singers.[5] By the early years of the new century, the stage was set for Vaughan to begin his own music company. A decision that had a far-reaching impact on the music industry. He began by publishing his first music book, *Gospel Chimes*, a compilation that included his original compositions, as well as the standard works of other musicians.

With his publishing venture in place, Vaughan decided in 1910 to dispatch a quartet to the conventions taking place across the country to sing and advertise his company's products. This turned out to be a huge success, and became the company pattern for many years, with as many as 16 quartets traveling the country representing the Vaughan Company. It also gave impetus for the rapid growth of gospel quartets throughout the South. The growing success of singing conventions also provided a fertile field of artistic expression and experimentation. Conventions were organized on a local, regional, and national level, with the first national singing convention held in 1936.[6] Vaughan expanded his company's use of media and by 1921 produced recordings through Vaughan Phonograph Records. In 1923 Vaughan began broadcasting on radio, eventually reaching the West coast and Canada.[7]

Virgil Stamps

One of Vaughan's Texas representatives, Virgil Stamps, left the Vaughan Company in 1924 and founded V.O. Stamps Music Company and V.O. Stamps School of Music. Stamps soon joined forces with Jesse Randall Baxter, Jr., and established the Stamps–Baxter Music Company in 1927.[8] A versatile Creative, Stamps was a singer, publisher, and songwriter. Baxter had worked for the A. J. Showalter Company prior to joining Stamps. They were able to secure the best talent of the day, employing well-known teachers such as William E. Combs in the Music School.[9] Over time, Stamps–Baxter became the most recognized name in the industry.

Stamps–Baxter quartets also traveled to the numerous singing conventions that were held across the country at that time. In 1936, Stamps–Baxter began broadcasting programs on radio that reached most of America and in 1938 inaugurated the "All Night Singing", a culminating event for students who had attended the music school, as well as other singing groups. In 1940, a group of 7,500 people attended the event in Texas.[10] While the Stamps–Baxter Music Company held a prominent place in Southern Gospel music at that time, other music companies were involved with the genre as well. According to historian James R. Goff, some of the more well known of these companies included the Teacher's Music Publishing Company (North Carolina), Morris–Henson Company (Georgia), Athens Music Company (Alabama), John Benson Publishing Company (Nashville), Trio Music Company (Texas), Central Music Company (Arkansas), and Tennessee Music and Printing Company (Tennessee).[11]

> **A versatile Creative, Virgil Stamps was a singer, publisher, and songwriter.**

Southern Gospel Creatives

Initially, Southern Gospel quartets and groups depended on music publishing companies, and yet, over time, became independent professional entities traveling the country to perform. With varying degrees of success, these Creatives changed with the times, utilizing venues like churches, camp meetings, singing conventions, secular concerts, radio, and television to spread the Southern gospel music genre. While the list of groups is extensive, some of the most well-known would include the Vaughan Quartet (1910), The Speer Quartet (1921), The Lefevres (1921), Stamps–Baxter Quartet (1924), The Chuck Wagon Gang (early 1930s), The Lesters (1930s), Blackwood Brothers Quartet (1934), Homeland Harmony Quartet (1935), Happy Goodmans (1940s), Sego Brothers/Sego Brothers and Naomi (1946), Florida Boys (1947), Statesmen Quartet (1948), The Jordanaires, (1948), The Kingsmen (1950s), Wendy Bagwell and the Sunliters (1950s), The Gaither Trio(1956), The Hoppers (1957), Cathedral Quartet (1964), and The Hinsons (1967).[12]

> As a leading Creative in the Gospel genre, Bill Gaither has been active in the field since the late 50s.

In recent years, new talent has been added to the roster, thanks in part to the mentoring role of Bill Gaither, bringing fresh inspiration and innovation. As a leading Creative in the Southern Gospel genre, Gaither has been active in the field since the late 50s. He, along with his wife Gloria, are multiple Grammy and Dove Award winners, and have helped shape both Southern Gospel and Contemporary Christian music for decades. Their resume of songs include, among many others, such classics as "The King Is Coming," "He Touched Me," and "It Is Finished."[13]

Gospel Music Creatives

Charles Albert Tindley

As Southern Gospel developed, so did the gospel music genre, building on the foundational work of two multitalented Creatives—Charles Albert Tindley and Thomas Andrew Dorsey. Born in 1851, Charles Albert Tindley, who was an accomplished speaker and songwriter, became one of the most well-known ministers of his day, pastoring a church of approximately 7,000 in Philadelphia. Tindley wrote songs such as "Nothing Between," "Leave It There," "We'll Understand It Better By And By," and "Stand By Me."[14] One of his most famous songs, "We Shall Overcome," became the theme song of the civil rights movement. Tindley was inducted into the Gospel Music Hall of Fame in 1993.[15]

Thomas Andrew Dorsey and Gospel Music

Born in Villa Rica, Georgia in 1899, Thomas Andrew Dorsey is considered the "Father of Gospel Music" within the Gospel Music tradition.[16] Dorsey was a pioneering musician who was a director, composer, singer, and pianist. In 1919, Dorsey began writing gospel songs, with his first hit coming in 1926 with "If You See My Savior, Tell Him That You Saw Me."[17]

In 1931, Dorsey and Theodore Frye created the first Black gospel chorus, which was foundational to the creation of the National Convention of Gospel Choirs and Choruses in 1933.[18] In the years ahead, gospel choirs would take on a significant role in churches across the country.

Born in Villa Rica, Georgia in 1899, Thomas Andrew Dorsey is considered the "Father of Gospel Music" within the Black gospel tradition.

"Precious Lord, Take My Hand," which came out in 1932, was written after the death of Dorsey's wife and son. With a musical style influenced by hymns, jazz, and blues, Dorsey established his own music studio and publishing company in 1932.[19] Prominent singers who worked with Dorsey included Mahalia Jackson, Della Reese, and Clara Ward.[20] In 1985, Dorsey was given the Governor's Award for the Arts and in 1992 received a Grammy National Trustees Award.[21]

James Cleveland

Grammy Award winning gospel artist, James Cleveland, was born in Chicago in 1931 and attended Pilgrim Baptist Church, where Thomas Dorsey served as minister of music and Roberta Martin was pianist. As a multitalented composer, musician, and singer, Cleveland showed a propensity for music at an early age and soon learned to sing and play the piano. In 1950, he joined with Norsalus McKissick and Bessie Folk to create the Gospelaires.[22] In 1967, Cleveland formed the Gospel Music Workshop of America (GMWA), an organization that convenes a wide array of musicians, performers, songwriters, and leaders throughout America. With 75,000 members and 185 chapters, GMWA has become an international organization.[23]

Mahalia Jackson, the Queen of Gospel Music
©Library of Congress, Prints & Photographs Division, Carl Van Vechten Collecton, LCUSZ62-120855

Mahalia Jackson

Known as the Queen of Gospel Music, Mahalia Jackson rose from poverty in Louisiana to be one of the most renowned singers of the twentieth century. Early on Jackson worked with Thomas A. Dorsey and popularized many of his songs. Jackson sang for John F. Kennedy's presidential inauguration and participated in Martin Luther King's march on Washington in 1963. After her death, Jackson was awarded a Lifetime Achievement Grammy.[24]

Kirk Franklin & The Comedy Gospel Tour
©Robb D. Cohen/Retna Ltd./Corbis

Numerous Creatives began careers individually and as groups in the genre over the twentieth century. Although this is not an exhaustive directory, a partial list would include The Fairfield Four (1921), The Dixie Hummingbirds (1928), Golden Gate Quartet (1930s), Mahalia Jackson (1930s), Blind Boys of Alabama (1939), The Sensational Nightingales (1942), Angelic Gospel Singers (1944), The Green Brothers/Al Green (1950s), The Caravans (1951), Mighty Clouds of Joy (1955), The Clara Ward Singers (1962), Aretha Franklin (1960s), The Andrews Gospel Singers (1960s), Andrea Crouch and the Disciples (1964), The Brooklyn Tabernacle Choir (1973), Mississippi Mass Choir (1988), Yolanda Adams (1988),[25] and Kirk Franklin (early 2000s).[26]

Big Band and Precursor to Contemporary Christian Music

Ralph Carmichael

The changes that took place in Christian music during the 1970s actually had precedent nearly a quarter century earlier in the music of Ralph Carmichael, one of the first musicians of the twentieth century to attempt creating contemporary Christian music for the public. Carmichael's efforts took place during a time when the musical taste of many churchgoers was formed by hymns and gospel music. As early as the 1940s, Carmichael was using the "Big Band" sound, so popular at that time, in the music he wrote and performed. His work incorporated trumpets, trombones, saxophones, flutes, clarinets, horns, keyboard, bass, drums, and guitars. While attending a Christian college in California, he produced a television show, The Campus Christian Hour, incorporating this style of music and eventually won an Emmy Award for his efforts.[27]

Carmichael went on to have a stellar career and worked for some of the most acclaimed personalities of that time including Pat Boone, Nat King Cole, Bing Crosby, and Ella Fitzgerald, and composed music for television. Light Records, which was formed by Carmichael, was at the forefront of making Christian Music available from the earliest days of the movement.[28] Carmichael helped bring many of the early Jesus Movement Creatives and art forms to the public.

In 1965, he created *Good News*, one of the first Christian musicals featuring pop and rock music.[29] In that same year, Andraé Crouch formed Andraé Crouch and the Disciples. In 1968, Crouch met Ralph Carmichael and produced the album *Take the Message Everywhere*.[30] Crouch has been one of the most successful Christian artists of the century, performing around the world and winning numerous awards for his music.

Gospel Music Artist Andraé Crouch Arrives at Dionne Warwick 45th Anniversary Special
©Axel Koester/Corbis

Contemporary Christian Music

While not without controversy, a paradigm shift took place in the 60s and 70s in the musical expression and consumption of many young Christians. As early as the 1950's, Thurlow Spurr began introducing contemporary instruments such as drums and electric guitars to his gospel songs. By 1964, Ray Repp used folk music in his *Mass for Young Americans*, which was performed in Catholic churches.[31] Also in 1964, the Salvation Army group The Joystrings came on the national stage in the United Kingdom with the pop song "Its An Open Secret." In 1967, Mind Garage, a band from Morgantown, West Virginia, began performing the *Electric Liturgy* for church services. According to the band's website, they performed the first known Christian Rock worship service in the world at Trinity Episcopal Church on March 10, 1968.[32] It is also possible that the term "theo-rock" was first used to describe the group's style and perhaps the new genre in general, at this time.[33]

In 1968, Agape and the All Saved Freak Band, two of the first hard rock Christian bands, were formed. Agape played at live events and produced their debut album *Gospel Hard Rock* in 1971. The group's sound has been compared to Jimi Hendrix, with possible influences of Grand Funk Railroad.[34] All Saved Freak Band used a blend of folk, rock, and blues to convey their message. Their debut album, *My Poor Generation*, was released in 1973. Other albums included *For Christians, Elves and Lovers* and *Brainwashed*, both released in 1976.[35]

Larry Norman, considered by some to be the father of Contemporary Christian music, began his career in the 1960s. In 1969, Norman released the first Christian rock album, *Upon This Rock*. He would go on to create *Only Visiting This Planet* (1972), *So Long Ago the Garden* (1973), and *In Another Land* (1976).[36] At the same time, Mylon Lefevre, of the Southern Gospel group The Singing Lefevres, switched genres to create one of the first Christian rock albums, releasing *Mylon* in 1970.[37]

Randy Stonehill, another early pioneer of the Contemporary Christian Music movement, released *Born Twice*, a rock album, in 1971. Stonehill went on to produce other albums as well.[38] Another influential Creative of the early years of the movement was Keith Green, a multitalented singer, pianist, and songwriter. His debut album, *For Him Who Has Ears to Hear*, was released in 1977. Green is best remembered for his devotional prose and "sold-out" Christian lifestyle. His music foreshadowed the transparent, prayer-like lyrics that distinguish the Praise and Worship music movement that would come later. Green was killed in a plane crash in 1982.

The 1970s were a time for pioneers of the new Christian music genre, which became a signature part of the Jesus Movement. Blending styles such as country, rock, folk, rhythm, blues, and jazz, these artists explored new ways of expressing their faith to the culture. This included the folk rock band Love Song, which formed in 1970 at California based Calvary Chapel, pastored by Chuck Smith. This church would later create Maranatha! Music, which has grown to be a major producer of Christian music since the beginning of the Jesus Movement. The group released their debut album *Love Song* in 1972.

Love Song's work had a major influence on early Jesus Music and with future artists in Contemporary Christian Music.[39] One of the longest running and at times most popular Christian rock bands from the 1970s was Petra, which formed in 1972. Other artists from the decade included The Archers, Daniel Amos, Phil Keaggy, Randy Matthews, The Resurrection Band, Children of the Day, Second Chapter of Acts, Sweet Comfort Band, Bethlehem, DeGarmo and Key, Gentle Faith, David and the Giants, Dallas Holmes and Praise, Barry McGuire, Noel Paul Stookey, and Nancy Honeytree.

The founding of *Contemporary Christian Music* magazine (later called CCM) in 1978 foreshadowed a diversification of the field.

The founding of Contemporary Christian Music magazine (later called CCM) in 1978 foreshadowed a diversification of the field.

By the beginning of the 1980s, changes in style were on the horizon. While the rock/metal sound did not disappear, evidenced by the popularity of groups like Petra, The Resurrection Band, Stryper, Bloodgood, Whitecross, and Bride at that time, the pop genre would further diversify Contemporary Christian music. One of the most influential artists of this time, Amy Grant, epitomized the culturally relevant Christian musician. Grant has had a long and very successful career in both the secular and Christian markets. Beginning in the early '80s, her hits included "Sing Your Praise to the Lord," "El Shaddai," "Emmanuel," and "Thy Word." Grant's crossover music has included "Baby, Baby," "Every Heartbeat," and "House of Love."[40]

Steven Curtis Chapman at the 51st Annual GRAMMY Awards. Staples Center, Los Angeles, CA. 02-08-09
©s_bukley/depositphotos

Michael W. Smith, who played backup keyboards for Amy Grant in the early 80s was a writer, musician, author, and consummate professional. In 1990, his song "Place in this World" was a crossover hit and went to number five on the pop music charts, as well as earning the New Artist of the Year award from the American Music Awards. Smith has won numerous accolades for his music, among them 40 Dove Awards.[41]

Steven Curtis Chapman, who came to the forefront of Christian music in the late 1980s, has helped shape the genre for decades. Chapman is a versatile artist who plays the guitar and piano, as well as composing songs. His first major work came in 1987 with "Weak Days" on his debut album *First Hand*.[42] As an artist, Chapman has set the standard in Christian music for years, winning 57 Dove awards, the most of any artist, as well as five Grammys, 47 number one singles, and nearly 11 million albums sold.[43]

Other artists of the decade included NewSong, Kathy Troccolli, Sandi Patti, The Imperials, Steve Taylor, Rich Mullins, Russ Taff, Twila Paris, Michael English, Wayne Watson, BeBe and CeCe Winans, Carman, The 77s, Charlie Peacock, Margaret Becker, Al Denson, Kim Hill, John Elefante, Scott Wesley Brown, Andrus, Blackwood & Company, Steve Camp, Brown Bannister, and Steve Green.

In the 90s, Christafari and DC Talk were two of the first groups to bring the sound of reggae, rap, and hip hop as subgenres to contemporary Christian music. Other significant artists from the decade included Jars of Clay, Point of Grace, Third Day, and Avalon. Today Creatives such as Lacrae, Switchfoot, TobyMac, Needtobreathe, Newsboys, Casting Crowns, Sanctus Real, Jeremy Camp and MercyMe top the charts and feature wide ranging styles and talent.

Festivals and Concerts

Cultural shifts in the 1970s found expression in a variety of media, but perhaps none more influential than music. The American public at this time had its share of religious themed songs performed by pop artists as diverse as Elvis Presley, Tennessee Ernie Ford, Judy Collins, B.J. Thomas, and Johnny Cash. At the same time, songs dealing with issues of war, rebellion, and the establishment were voiced in the chart topping hits of the day. Yet another group, initially known as "Jesus Music" artists, began shaping the cultural landscape as well, developing outdoor and indoor festivals and concerts.

Large outdoor festivals, such as Woodstock, were common across the nation in the late 60s and early 70s and were a format used by both secular and Christian groups alike. Christian festivals featured the Creatives of the fledgling field known variously as Jesus Music, Jesus Rock, Christian Rock, and Contemporary Christian Music. Music festivals among Christians had precedent in the early holiness and camp meetings held at the turn of the century.

Faith Festival, held in 1970, was one of the first Christian festivals of this genre. Organized by Youth for Christ, approximately 6,000 people came to hear musicians such as Pat Boone, Danny Taylor, and Larry Norman.[44] The Ichthus Festival began in 1970 as well and is considered to be the longest running Christian music festival in the country. Ichthus has featured some of the most well-known Christian groups in America. Each year around 20,000 people attended the festival. In 2013, Ichthus became a part of the Creation Festivals.[45]

Numerous interdenominational festivals grew up across the nation during the 70s and provided an artistic springboard for new Creatives. The Love Song Festival in 1971, Explo '72, the Jesus Festival in 1973, Praise '74, Jesus '75, Salt '75, Fishnet '75, and Sonshine Festival '75, just to name a few.[46] In 1979, Creation Festivals was founded by Harry Thomas and Tim Landis and has grown to be one of the largest of its type in the nation. Numerous artists have appeared at Creation Festivals including Chuck Girard, Larry Norman, The Resurrection Band, Amy Grant, The Newboys, DC Talk, Burlap to Cashmere, Phil Keaggy, TobyMac, Chris Tomlin, Switchfoot, Skillet, and Hawk Nelson.[47]

While many of the festivals featured up-and-coming talent as well as more established Creatives, some were intended for musicians exclusively. The Christian Artists' Seminar, held at Estes Park in Colorado, was founded in 1975 by Cam Floria.[48]

Three singers leading worship
©Ron Nickel/Design Pics/Corbis

By 1996, Gary Gentry and Roy Morgan founded Premiere Festivals to promote numerous festivals around the country. The North Carolina based organization promotes music festivals such as Beach Blast in Myrtle Beach, South Carolina; Christian Music Day and JoyFest at Carowinds in Charlotte, North Carolina; Wonder Jam in Canada; Spirit Song at Kings Island, Ohio; PointFest in Sandusky, Ohio; and WinterFest, held at Liberty University in Lynchburg, Virginia.[49]

Within the first decade of the new millennium, the Christian Festivals Association, consisting of 21 member festivals from across the nation, was founded. Member organizations include AgapeFest, Alive Festival, AtlantaFest, Big Ticket Festival, East to West Festival, Elevate Festival, FISHFEST, Fandana Festival, Hills Alive, Kingdom Bound, King's Fest, LifeLight Festivals, Lifest, Rock The Desert, Rock The Island, SoulFest, SpiritSong Festival, Spirit West Coast, Unity Christian Music Festival, and Uprise Festival. Over three-quarters of a million people attend Creation Festivals annually.[50]

Contemporary Praise and Worship

The development of contemporary worship music has paralleled the changes that initially took place with the Jesus Movement. Both Protestant and Catholic churches have been influenced by these changes. Calvary Chapel, located in Costa Mesa, California, was one of the first churches to utilize this type of music in worship. Communal singing among churches at the time was generally built around a choir, traditional hymns, and musical instruments such as the piano or organ. Jesus Movement Creatives composed original music for worship that included the styles expressed in popular culture at the time, generally sung by an individual, small group, or band.

In the 1970s, Love Song was one of the first groups to compose praise music for worship.[51] Maranatha! Music, a ministry of Calvary Chapel, was created in order to make this music available to churches.[52] Vineyard Music and Integrity Music were also developed early in the movement and provided new music to the church.[53] Over time, terms such as "worship team," worship band," and "praise team" have been used to describe the role of these Creatives in worship.

Praise and Worship music has become an international phenomenon. Many examples could be cited, but two in particular stand out. In 1995, the Passion Movement was established by Louie Giglio to enable students to follow the call of Christ. A major component of the movement has been music, featuring artists such as David Crowder, Chris Tomlin, Kristian Stanfill, Matt Redman, and Matt Maher.[54] Established in 1983, Hillsong Church, headquartered in Australia with sites located in 12 countries, has become one of the major centers for Praise Music Creatives, including work by internationally acclaimed songwriter and worship leader Darlene Zschech.[55]

Classical Music

Another facet of the music field was being influenced during the 70s as well, and while starting as only a dream, has had an international influence. Sensing a call to minister to classical musicians, three couples from the Washington, DC area, Dr. Patrick and Barbara Kavanaugh, Dr. Jim and Mary Jeane Kraft, and Bob and Robin Sturm, founded the Classical Performing Artists Fellowship in 1984. The vision for this ministry actually began in the 1970s, when the Kavanaughs and Krafts felt led to begin a ministry to those involved in classical performing arts. Today, the CPAF is a "trans-denominational ministry dedicated to performing and teaching the classical arts to the glory of God and to spreading the gospel of Jesus Christ."[56]

MasterWorks Festival, a four-week music, dance, and theatre festival, is sponsored by CPAF and is held each year at Grace College. Students learn from accomplished Creatives from a variety of performing arts disciplines.[57] Drawing students from around the world, Masterworks Festival offers programs in Orchestra and Chamber Music Studies, Piano, Wind Intensive Study, String Intensive Study, Vocal Intensive Study, Ballet and Modern Dance, Theater, Technical Internships, Choral and Conducting programs.[58]

The preceding examples are indicative of movements within the field of music intended to express the message of the gospel. Using a variety of styles, media, and venues, these Creatives have been heard by millions of people around the world. Others with the same goal were also intent on using another form of expression, visual art. As will be seen, the twentieth century was a time when visual arts Creatives intent on expressing their faith to the Church and culture, used a wide range of art forms and media such as cartoons, paintings, architecture, film, and animation.

Pioneer Creative Catalyst's Story

Bill Drake,
Director of OM Arts International

Abused and unwanted as a child and young teenager, Bill Drake knows what it is to feel hurt, rejected and without hope. At the age of 19 he was playing piano in bars and nightclubs in his native America and was on the brink of ending what he describes as his "unlovely life." Then a group of young people decided to step out of their comfort zone and witness to Bill and others like him. They challenged him not to take his life, but to lose it, to give it up to the God who loved him unconditionally and who could give his life the purpose it had never had. Bill remembers walking home one night, feeling like he had a gun in one hand and a Bible in the other. A choice needed to be made.

By the grace of God, he chose to die – to self. God radically changed his life and began to use his musical gifting to challenge and encourage many others. Several years later George Verwer, founder of the international mission organization Operation Mobilization, heard Bill lead worship at Biola University in California and threw out a challenge: "How can you play and sing songs like that if you are not willing to back it up with your lifestyle?" Bill was stunned. This total stranger had just seen right through all Bill's pretense and hypocrisy. George went on to challenge Bill to live the commitment he was singing about and join Operation Mobilization as International Music Minister. After graduating from Biola, Bill did this, living in England for 10 years with his wife Teri and their two daughters, Shelby and Sharayah.

An ordained minister, skilled musician and gifted preacher and teacher, Bill Drake has been privileged to minister in over 50 countries. Many have recognized an anointing on Bill's music similar to that on Keith Green's, and thousands of lives have been touched and radically changed through Bill's powerful music and uncompromising message which continues to make the life-changing message of God's love a reality. Bill has released a number of recordings, including As I Come Into Your Presence, and Wear The Crown, and released his new album Broken&Complete in September 2012, his thirteenth album of original music.

In 2009 Bill helped to found and was appointed Director of OM Arts International, the creative arts ministry of Operation Mobilization International. Partnering with other leaders in OM who were engaged in Dance, Drama, Visual Arts, Music, and Ethnodoxology, Bill and team forged a unique ministry within the larger fellowship of OM, actively engaging with local believers in bringing the Gospel of Jesus Christ in many countries in Europe, the Middle East, and around the world.

OM Arts facilitates artists of all kinds into missions through short-term trips, long-term placement, and missionary training at "Incarnate" – the OM Arts School of Mission. "I felt it was time to give back", says Bill, about founding OM Arts. "I have been afforded such unbelievable opportunities to serve all over the world through the arts, and have seen their undeniable impact on lives and communities. All peoples of the earth express their worldview and their deepest longings through their art forms, and to engage with them at this level is one of the most powerful ways in which we can demonstrate and communicate the love of God and the Gospel of the Kingdom."

Bill Drake lives with his wife Teri in Atlanta, Georgia, and holds a B.A. in Christian Education from Biola University, and a Masters Degree in Worship Studies from the Institute for Worship Studies in Jacksonville, Florida.
www.billdrake.com | www.arts.om.org

Pioneer Creative Catalyst's Story

Dr. Frank Fortunato,
Founder, Heart Sounds International, Operation Mobilization Vice President, International Council of Ethnodoxologists

Dr. Frank Fortunato began his music missions career serving on the mission ships of Operation Mobilization. At any one time on the ships, the crew and staff came from 30-40 nations. It was during this time that Fortunato tapped into this global community and helped develop international evenings of song, dance and folklore that became the culminating events for each of the port visits. In more open countries a ship speaker gave a Christian message and people in each port responded to the invitation to receive Christ. He also led worship at the OM global conferences and included multicultural worship in these events. This, in turn, led to his involvement at global mission conferences where he helped organize worship, special music in various languages, and compiled multilingual songbooks for these events.

The growing interest in multicultural worship led to the creation of music and the arts task forces with agencies including the World Evangelical Alliance

Mission Commission, the International Orality Network, and OM's Heart Sounds International, a ministry devoted to helping people groups release biblically appropriate and culturally relevant worship recordings that reflected their indigenous music expressions. Fortunato did undergraduate studies in piano, a Masters in Ethnomusicology and completed a doctorate in Worship Studies from the Robert E. Webber Institute for Worship Studies. Following completion of doctoral studies, Fortunato co-taught courses on cross-cultural worship at the Institute, and was appointed the director of Webber Institute GROW (Global Renewal of Worship) Center. He serves as the international worship consultant for OM, and as a arts in mission advocate with various global Christian networks.

Fortunato is also the Vice President of The International Council of Ethnodoxologists (ICE), the Coordinator of Missional Relations for the Webber Institute, and directs the Institute's GROW Center. He is the founder of OM's Heart Sounds International, a ministry producing indigenous worship recordings, mostly in the restricted parts of the world. Fortunato co-authored *All the World is Singing—Glorifying God through the worship music of the nations*, and co-edited *Worship and Mission for the Global Church-an Ethnodoxology Handbook*. The Fortunatos are based at the OM USA headquarters in Atlanta, Georgia.

Pioneer Creative Catalyst's Story

Ralph Carmichael,
Composer, Contemporary Christian Music Pioneer

Followers of Christ have an assignment known as "The Great Commission." Simply stated, it means to take the message of salvation to the whole world. The problem is that down through the years there has often been disagreement as to just what "ways and means" could be used to spread this marvelous message to a lost world. I remember hearing about how a printer during the pilgrim holiness days back on the East coast was run out of town when he used the press to duplicate passages of scripture to be distributed to nonbelievers. They claimed the printing press was of the devil and could not be used to spread the gospel. Close to home and as recent as the 1930s, my father had to cope with a similar barrier. Dad was pastoring a church in Fargo, North Dakota. He arranged for the church to sponsor a weekly radio on a station located across the river in Moorhead, Minnesota. Shortly after he went on the air, the deacons told him he could not use church funds to broadcast because the radio was the devils "little black box". Dad stayed on the air and paid for the airtime out of his own pocket.

Now, fast forward to the late 40s and I'm in my late teens and attending Southern California Bible College in Pasadena, California. I enrolled there in Summer School in 1944, directly after high school graduation. I began fulfilling a dream by organizing various musical groups of young students there. The first was a male quartet, then a female trio, which I put together and had a septet, and eventually added another female and had an octet. Then I began experimenting with what they called "close harmony". Next came a trumpet trio, and then a big leap to an eight-piece brass choir with four trumpets and four trombones. I had grown up listening to the big bands that were popular at the time, for example Harry James, Tommy Dorsey, Benny Goodman and Duke Ellington.

I thought "my oh my how wonderful it would be to have a big band that played Gospel music." It wasn't long till I found some fellow students who had played saxophone in their high school marching band. I found two alto sax players and three tenors, but no baritone sax. Then one of the tenors said, "If you'll give me a berry, I'll learn how to play it." I already had my eight-piece brass, and a four-man rhythm section–that would be an upright base, an acoustic guitar, keyboard and drums. Now, if I could find a baritone sax, I would have a five-piece saxophone section. At about that time I was hired as the choir director at the Englewood Assembly of God Church and received a small weekly salary, which I used to rent a baritone sax from a music store in downtown Los Angeles.

The next week I had my first big band rehearsal on the campus of Southern California Bible College. The rehearsal took place in a basement classroom beneath the college offices and the noise was not appreciated. I remember two things that happened. One was that future rehearsals would have to take place a block down from the campus in the gymnasium. The second was that the baritone sax could not be kept on campus. Why? Because it was a dance band instrument and was evil. I could still use it in the band, but it had to be kept off campus. Well, I found a fifth year student who lived a mile or so off campus who agreed it and bring it on Monday, Wednesday and Friday to our rehearsals.

Soon we were doing concerts around Southern California and I was flunking classes because I would stay up all night writing arrangements for the band. One of the concerts took place in a big church in Pasadena for a men's fellowship and afterwards a gentleman came up and mentioned that we should be on television. He was the owner of a company that manufactured and sold baby carriages. I soon heard from his advertising agency and we were on TV with a program called "The Campus Christian Hour." We signed to do just one show. The president of the college called me in when he heard about it and said, "OK, you can do this, we'll pay for the transportation and let you take the students off campus, but you have to agree to one thing. You cannot mention the name of the college on the air."

You see, at that time television was considered a very worldly thing. I agreed to his request and the "Campus Christian Hour" went on the air. After we did the first show, they got so much mail–believe it or not some of it was hate mail. Some of it had to do with the fact that we went on as Christians but were on television with a big band. But the station didn't mind that it wasn't good mail. The fact that they got a lot of attention made them want us to do more television. And so we did, we signed to do three shows, then thirteen. Someone nominated us for an Emmy, imagine that, and in 1949 we won! I have a picture hanging on my wall of Governor Earl Warren presenting us with the Emmy award. Two days later, there was a note in my letterbox on campus from the president of the college asking me to meet him in his office at my earliest convenience. I thought I was in for it now. That afternoon I walked into his office and he said, "Have a seat." I thought "oh boy, I'm going to get it now." He told me he had heard about the award and congratulated me. Then, with a big grin on his face he said, " You know, since we're paying for the gas, and letting you take the students out of class and off campus to do that television show, the least you could do is give the college some credit during the show." Well, we did. The very next show, we had signs posted all over the stage that credited the location as Southern California Bible College Campus.

The show ran for a total of 78 weeks. One of my guests was Dr. Billy Graham, for whom I was writing film scores. Some of those early films were tailored for and directed at the teen audience. One of the songs I wrote was "He's Everything to Me" and in the film the song was sung by a group of teens around a bonfire on the beach. A rhythm section playing even eight notes with a gentle rock-n-roll beat accompanied them. That was the beginning of an experiment to reach out to young people with the gospel message using a musical form they would listen to. We wrote, published and recorded several youth musicals including Tell It Like It Is and Natural High. At that same time we did an adult Christmas musical Specially For Shepherds, using a contemporary orchestral accompaniment.

In the 50s the Lord opened several doors of opportunity. I was hired as minister of music at Temple Baptist Church, headquartered in the Los Angeles Philharmonic auditorium. One day the pastor informed me that the church had plans for a two-week revival for which I would like you to write a new song of invitation. That is when I wrote "A Savior Is Waiting" and used it as the invitation after every sermon. Dr. Bob Pierce of World Vision was visiting us one night and heard the song. The following day he asked to be the music director for a 30-day revival in Tokyo, Japan, which would include a large choir and full symphony orchestra nightly. At the close of each sermon, he asked me to use "The Savior Is Waiting" as the song of invitation. We printed copies of the song to pass out to the audience with lyrics in both English and Japanese. We were visited by hundreds of clergy members from the United States. While in Tokyo I recorded an album called " One Hundred and Two Strings" and actually had that many players on the album. What a dream come true!

In the months following, I began to get requests from publishers for licenses to publish the song and today "The Savior Is Waiting" is in many hymnals worldwide. The next exciting experiment was an album called "Rhapsody In Sacred Music" recorded for Sacred Records at Capital Records Studio A. Next came an acapella album using 25 of the top studio singers in Hollywood, made up of six sopranos, six altos, six tenors, and seven basses. The extra basses name was Thurl Ravenscroft. The album was first released on the Sacred Records label called "Garden of the Heart". It was released again on Light Records and called The Savior Is Waiting." To sum up an exciting 60 years of musical ministry, let me say that innovation and experiment have come with a lot of criticism, but I'll tell you this, it has been worth it. When I was growing up as a teenager, my folks had a motto that hung on the kitchen wall, and I'd like to leave you with it. It was a little two-line poem written by a missionary pioneer named C. T. Studd that goes like this:

" Only one life, twill soon be past,
Only what's done for Christ will last."

I pray to Lord that every note I write is not for me, it is to spread the Gospel and to glorify Christ.

FIVE

Visual Arts

"Protestants are beginning to wonder if their God
is not the same now that he was when he found Bezaleel the son of Uri
and 'filled him with the Spirit of God, in wisdom, and in understanding,
and in knowledge, and in all manner of workmanship…'"
—HENRY TURNER BAILEY
1904

Perspective view, northeast, of Ira Allen Chapel on the campus of the University of Vermont. This Colonial Revival chapel was designed by McKim, Mead, and White in 1925.
Courtesy of Library of Congress

The Creatives who worked in the visual arts during the twentieth century were influenced by the trends of the time, but also looked to the future with innovative intuition. Changing economic, social, political, and religious conditions on the national and international stage helped Creatives determine what to design and build. The century also witnessed the steady development both inside and outside denominations of para-church organizations with varying roles in the process.

Architecture

Among its many purposes in culture, the Church building serves as a visual symbol and communicates the ideals and aspirations of the Christian community. Thousands of churches were built over the century in a variety of styles, the major purpose being to provide form and function for the public act of communal worship. Along with the edifice movement was a steady development, both inside and outside denominations, of architectural offices and leaders with varying roles in the church building process. Several examples serve to illustrate the growing trend toward organization-wide building efforts.

Within the first decade of the twentieth century, the Young Men's Christian Association had established an architectural bureau, followed in 1916 by the creation of the Department of Architecture within the Southern Baptist Church. One year later in 1917, the Joint Committee on Architecture was created in the Methodist Episcopal Church to direct denominational construction. After WWI, The Lutheran Church, Missouri Synod, created The Committee on Church Architecture in 1922.[1]

Denominational leaders in the first half of the twentieth century overseeing these offices were determined to improve church design and building practices. Their efforts laid the foundation for what would take place for decades to come. Ralph Adams Cram and Eero Saarinen were architects whose ecclesiastical commissions would influence church building trends throughout the twentieth century. Other denominational Creatives concerned with the role of architecture gained prominence as well. Perhaps one of the most well-known advocates for architectural standards at this time, Elbert Conover, a Methodist minister, speaker, and writer, served over 30 years as the leader of Methodist Church's Joint Committee on Architecture.[2]

Conover's Lutheran counterpart, Frederick Webber, was a leading spokesman for the Lutheran Church, Missouri Synod's architectural program beginning in the 1920s. He wrote *Church Symbolism*, as well as a journal titled *Lutheran Church Art* (later *The Church Builder*). The Southern Baptist Sunday School Board Architectural Department was headed by R.E. Burroughs. Maurice Lavanoux, editor of *Liturgical Arts* and secretary of the Liturgical Arts Society, and Brother Cajetan, who became head of the Office of Franciscan Art and Architecture, would emerge as the major proponents for Catholic architectural practices related to liturgy and worship. Conover, Webber, Lavanoux, Cajetan, and their contemporaries viewed issues related to architectural style, design, and function as crucial factors in liturgy and worship.[3]

An early interdenominational effort, the North American Conference on Church Architecture and the Allied Arts was held in 1936 in New York, and by

Eero Saarinen designed many modern ecclesiastical commissions.
©Library of Congress, Prints & Photographs Division, Balthazar Korab Archive at the Library of Congress, LC-KRB00- I024

1940 the Church Architectural Guild of America (later Guild of Religious Architects) created the department.[4] By mid-century, the National Council of Churches came into being, with a department, the Bureau of Church Buildings and Architecture, headed by Elbert Conover, designed to address issues related to church architecture. In 1976, the Interfaith Forum on Religion, Art, and Architecture was formed as the result of a merger between several interdenominational organizations focused on art and architecture.[5]

The end of WWII also brought a renewed emphasis on building, as well as new leadership among denominational architecture departments. Catholics and Protestant denominations such as Southern Baptist, Disciples of Christ, United Methodist, Presbyterian Church, USA, United Lutheran Church in America, and Lutheran Church, Missouri Synod, began to actively develop plans to meet congregational building needs, resulting in the construction of thousands of churches.

From mid-century till the 2000s, churches of all sizes and types, from megachurch to chapel, have used a number of architectural styles including Gothic Revival, Colonial Revival, Romanesque Revival, Spanish Revival, Pueblo Revival, Greek Revival, Modern, International Style, and Modern Gothic, just to name a few.[6]

Liturgical Arts

The Catholic Liturgical Renewal Movement had close connections to church architecture, influencing Catholic institutions in particular at all levels, and eventually other mainline Protestant churches interested in renewing connections to their liturgical heritage. In the visual arts, leaders in organizations such as the Liturgical Arts Society, the Catholic Art Association and the Office of Franciscan Art and Architecture worked to integrate the principles of renewal and inform constituents about issues related to art and the liturgy.[7] As early as 1929, the Society of Catholic Artists, originally known as the Guild of Catholic Artists and Craftsmen, was founded in the United Kingdom.[8] The Liturgical Arts Society, which was located in New York, began publishing a quarterly journal, *Liturgical Arts* in 1931. Each issue, distributed primarily in America, featured a variety of articles, illustrations, and designs related to the arts in the Catholic Church. Eventually Maurice Lavanoux, the tireless advocate for liturgical arts, became editor of *Liturgical Arts* and remained so until the Society ceased existence in 1972.

Over the years, distinguished artists and architects were associated with the group, such as Hildreth Meiere.[9] Meiere studied art in Florence, the Art Students League of New York, California School of Fine Arts, the Art Institute of Chicago, the New York School of Applied Design for Women and Beaux Arts Institute of Design. Meiere went on to become one of the most prominent mural artists in American history, executing numerous ecclesiastical and public commissions, including work for architects like Bertram Goodhue.[10]

An exhibit by Catholic artists organized in 1950 by the group Pax Romana would be the springboard for the creation of the International Society of Catholic Artists, now the International Society of Christian Artists. Five artists in the exhibit, Lambert and Ineke Simon, Christof Wintemitz, Helene Koller-Buchwiser and Ferdinand Pfamatter, met in 1951 and founded the organization as an affiliate of Pax Romana. Since its founding, the organization has held numerous conferences, workshops and exhibits.

> The Liturgical Arts Society, which was located in New York, began publishing a quarterly journal, Liturgical Arts in 1931. Each issue, distributed primarily in America, featured a variety of articles, illustrations, and designs related to the arts in the Catholic Church.

With its inaugural event in 2011, the Catholic Artists Society traces its impetus for existence to a homily by Pope Benedict XVI, the *Address to Artists*, held in the Sistine Chapel, in 2009. An intriguing element of the inaugural event, which was held at The Church of Our Saviour in New York, was the Mass of the Holy Spirit for Artists. In May of 2014, the organization held its annual

Mass for Artists in St. Patrick's Old Cathedral, marking the 15th Anniversary of Pope John Paul II's *Letter to Artists*. The organization states:

> Following the Holy Father's call for artists to be "custodians of Beauty" and "heralds and witnesses of Hope for humanity" the society seeks to encourage the ongoing artistic and spiritual development of artists and media professionals, so that their work may more perfectly reflect God's glory, enriching and ennobling men and women, our society and our culture.[11]

A Question of Style

By the 1950s, visual art forms in Catholic and Protestant churches, whether in the form of educational materials, sculpture, paintings, altars, or baptismal scenes, were predominately representational. However, Marvin Halverson and some of his associates questioned this style. As previously stated, Halverson was the Executive Director of the National Council of Church's (NCC) Department of Worship and the Arts until 1962, and actively promoted the arts within national denominations. Halverson, Alfred Barr, who was director of the Museum of Modern Art, and their associates advanced the thesis that representational art failed to communicate the message of the church to culture as effectively as modern art, more specifically abstract art. For Halverson and Barr, the writings of Paul Tillich, prominent mid-century philosopher and theologian, helped advance a theological aesthetic conducive to modern art.[12]

> ... the works of more contemporary Creatives such as Marc Chagall, Rudolph Schwartz, Andre Girard, Jean Charlot, Barry Byrne, Marcel Breuer and Georges Rouault were published in Liturgical Arts.

Through a series of publications, articles, lectures, and exhibits, Halverson and his group disseminated their aesthetic preferences. The work of Georges Rouault, for example, was preferred to that of Warner Sallman or Heinrich Hofmann.[13] Warner Sallman, who was at this time a noted painter of religious art, was best known for his painting the *Head of Christ*. At the same time, the works of more contemporary Creatives such as Marc Chagall, Rudolph Schwartz, Andre Girard, Jean Charlot, Barry Byrne, Marcel Breuer and Georges Rouault were published in *Liturgical Arts*.[14] Halverson led the Department of Worship and the Arts till 1962, eventually reconfigured within the NCC. Halverson left to continue work with the Society for Arts, Religion, and Contemporary Culture.[15] In the end, both realistic and abstract art styles became part of the milieu of art styles used by Christians to express their faith.

Visual Arts Organizations

As Halverson continued to develop SARCC, Eugene Johnson, who was an art professor at Bethel College, held a conference for Christian artists in 1977, with a follow-up conference in 1979 at Calvin College, at which Christians in the Visual Arts (CIVA) was founded. What began as a dream has expanded to become one of the major faith-based art organizations in America, with over 600 members. CIVA has a three-part mission, which includes a call to creative work, devotion to the Church, and the call to be present in culture. CIVA "[w]as born as a response to the absence of a tangible Christian community within the contemporary American art world. As it matured, CIVA grew to become a place of aesthetic stimulation and spiritual encouragement."[16] While it would be impossible to list all artists working with CIVA, the list would include Edward Cameron Wayne, Sadao Watanabe, Bruce Herman, Edward Knippers, Theodore Prescott, Sandra Bowden, Cliff McReynolds, and Cam Anderson.

Its long-range vision is to "help artists, arts pastors, collectors, critics, designers, filmmakers, historians, and theologians explore the profound relationship between art and faith."[17] Publications by CIVA have included *SEEN Journal, CIVA Sourcebook, CIVA Views, Faith+Vision*, and *The Next Generation*. The organization hosts a biennial conference and traveling exhibits throughout America.

By 2000, Episcopal Church Visual Arts (ECVA) was founded and now has chapters in California, Illinois, Maryland, Nevada, New Jersey, New York, North Carolina, Oklahoma, Pennsylvania, Texas, Vermont, and Washington State.[18]

Religious Education and Visual Art

Reform efforts occurring in America during the late nineteenth and early twentieth century affected instructional and curricular strategies in both public

Henry Turner Bailey and Students
©Chautauqua Institution Photographic Collection

and religious education, with many methods still in use today. Denominations throughout the country, influenced by the Sunday School movement, sought to improve the effectiveness of their message and, in many cases, Biblical paintings, original illustrations, photographs, and filmstrips were used to enhance lessons.

Both Catholic and Protestant churches alike included the visual arts in Sunday School lessons and on take home cards, all readily available through numerous publishing companies.

Groups such as the Religious Education Association met to consider a wide array of topics related to the topic. Early on, advocates such as Henry Turner Bailey, Waldo S. Pratt, Harriet Cecil Magee, and H. Augustine Smith recognized the role of visual arts in learning. Smith's book, *Worship in the Church School Through Music, Pageantry and Pictures*, proposed numerous uses of the arts, and of particular interest here the visual arts, in Sunday School.[19] Like many of his contemporaries, Smith saw the educational value of picture study as a means of art appreciation and spiritual formation. He recommended representational works for Sunday School by Armitage, Harrach, Siemiradski, Hole, Reynolds, Honthorst, Rembrandt, Zimmerman, Cornicelius, Brown, Copping, Eastlake, Millais, Poynter, Burnard, and others.[20]

Both Catholic and Protestant churches alike included the visual arts in Sunday School lessons and on take home cards, all readily available through numerous publishing companies. Religious literature, often tailored to evangelistic, theological and societal issues, included illustrations, cartoons and sequential Bible stories. Chalk-talk artists such Percy Kadey and Edwin Wallace traveled among churches illustrating Bible stories.[21]

Illustrators

Frank Beard

Born in 1842, Frank Beard was one of the major Christian artists of the nineteenth century. His major artistic contributions were in *Judge* and *The Ram's Horn*, eventually becoming principal illustrator, drawing single panel cartoons and comics. While Beard was most significant prior to the twentieth century, his pioneering work in the Chautauqua meetings as a "chalk talk" artist influenced multitudes of people across denominations through visual expression. His work anticipated the role of the visual arts, especially cartoons and comic books, which would develop in the next century.[22]

Ernest Pace

Ernest James Pace was born in the late nineteenth century and had widespread influence across denominations in America and abroad through the mid-twentieth century. Educated at Otterbein University and Princeton Seminary, where he earned the Doctor of Ministry degree, Pace was perhaps one of the most significant early twentieth century Christian comic artists. He began illustrating for the Chicago based *Journal* at the age of 19, and after graduating from college went to the Philippines with his wife for missions work. Over several years, he illustrated hundreds of cartoons for a denominational journal *The Watchword*. Around 1916, Pace began illustrating lessons for *The Sunday School Times*, which had a circulation of more than 100,000 including America and other countries. From 1917 to 1921, Pace taught at Moody Bible Institute. From the quarter century point till almost mid-century, Pace's illustrations appeared in *The Layman's League* and *Evangelical Christian*, in William Jennings Bryan's 1924 book *Seven Questions in Dispute*, as well as in *Christian Cartoons* and *Pictures That Talk* among others.[23]

Comic Book Artists

Al Hartley

Born in 1921, Al Hartley was a successful comic book artist and writer for both Christian and non-Christian companies. Early on he showed interest in art and took art lessons at the Art Students League of New York. Comic book publishers Hartley worked for were Atlas, Timely, Marvel, Standard, Quality, and American. His creative activities brought him in contact with celebrated comic artists such as Stan Lee and Jack Kirby. Hartley's major artistic contribution came after he became a Christian in 1967 and his subsequent work with Archie, Spire, and Barbour Comics, eventually creating approximately 60 Christian comics, with over 40 million copies sold.[24] Other significant comic artists could be listed as well. The following includes the artist, and approximate decade when started: Vaughan Shoemaker (1920s), Charles Ramsay (1930s), Jack Hamm (1940s), Phil Saint (1940s), Betty Russell (1940s), Greg Laurie (Maranatha! Publications, 1960s), Rick Griffin (1970s), Fred Carter (Chick Publications, 1970s), Donald Ensign (Cofounded Christian Comic Arts Society, 1980s), Ron Wheeler (1980s), Dick Hafer (1980s), Tom Finley (1980s), Kevin Frank (1980s), and Kathleen Webb (1980s).[25]

Comic Books

While not an all-inclusive list, numerous comic books have been produced over the span of the twentieth century including *Christian Cartoons* (Sunday School Times, 1922), *Gospel Cartoons* (Polzin Press, 1937), *The Life of Jesus Visualized* (1942, The Standard Publishing Company), *Tullus* (David C. Cook, 1943), *Bible Stories in Pictures* (Concordia Publishing House, 1947), *Sunday Pix* (David C. Cook Publishing Company, 1949), *Billy Graham Presents* Series (The Billy Graham Evangelistic Association/Grayson Company,1951–53), *Oral Roberts True Stories* and *Junior Partners* Series (Oral Roberts Evangelistic Association/Tele Pix, 1956/57, 59), *Run Baby Run* (Logos International/David C. Cook Publishing Company, 1971), *The Cross and the Switchblade / God's Smuggler /Archie* (Spire/Barbour, 1972), *The Crusaders* (Chick Publications,1974), *Merlin R. Carothers / Run Baby Run, Amazing Saints* and *Ben Israel* (Logos International, 1974).[26]

In the 1980s, Christian comic books included titles such as the *Heroes of Faith* Series (United Bible Society, 1982), *Cosmics* Series (Tyndale House, 1987), *Aida-*

Zee (The Nate Butler Studio, 1990), *Christian Crusader* Series (CC Comics, 1992), *Kidz of the King* (King Comics and KOTK Publishing, 1994), *Archangels: The Saga* (Eternal Studios, 1995), and *Proverbs & Parables* (New Creation Publications and the Christian Comic Arts Society, 1998).[27] In 1996, Nate Butler, who had worked with *Archie, Heathcliff* and *Snuffy Smith*, founded Christian Comics International. Later, several publishing activities led to the creation of COMIX35, which has provided consulting, coaching, and classes in 52 countries since being founded.[28]

> Since 2011, Zondervan released graphic novels The Book of Revelation, Kingdoms and Morningstar.

Since the early 2000s, a number of successful superhero movies have been released based on popular Marvel and DC Comic characters. At the same time, a new emphasis among Christian publishers included a style more reflective of modern comics. In 2010, David C. Cook Publishing Company released the best-selling Action Bible, which was illustrated by award winning artist Sergio Cariello.[29] Since 2011, Zondervan released graphic novels *The Book of Revelation, Kingdoms* and *Morningstar*.[30] In 2011, Art Ayris, CEO of Leesburg, Florida based Kingstone Media, began releasing comic books and graphic novels. Titles such as *Noah, Job, Samson, Moses*, and the *Christ* series have been created.[31] Lee Weeks, who has drawn comic characters for Marvel, DC, and Dark Horse Comics, created the cover for Kingstone Media's *Samson* title. Items are available on ComiXology, the largest comics app worldwide, Iverse Media, Kindle Fire, Kingstone Apple App for iPhone and iPad, Kingstone Android App and Nook.[32]

The Moving Image

In the early 1900s, an emerging visual art form, film, which built on the photographic art form, was viewed by certain branches of the church as a potential medium for evangelism, education, and entertainment, inaugurating a century long experiment with the moving image. According to Terry Lindvall, churches used film "to achieve their mission of attracting new audiences, of instructing and entertaining their congregations, and of exploiting nontheatrical films to serve the Kingdom of God and their parishes."[33]

Scene from The King of Kings
© Conde Nast Archives/Corbis

An organization that would grow to have an international impact actually began with the seminal meeting of 150 Evangelical leaders in 1944 to establish the National Religious Broadcasters (NRB). Early efforts were initially focused on radio; yet the organization grew over time to include television and other media. Reflecting the growing influence of the Christian media across the globe, the NRB now has affiliate organizations internationally including ACB Russia, Association of Christian Media Southern Africa, Christian Media Australia, COICOM (Spanish speaking countries), and Fellowship of European Broadcasters.[34]

By the early 50s, postwar America experienced a surge in church attendance, economic expansion, and nationalism. At around the same time, Ken Anderson created the Gospel Films Company and the Billy Graham Evangelistic Association founded World Wide Pictures. Other companies included Family

Films and Ken Anderson Films.[35] Within a decade of Gospel Films and World Wide Pictures being created, the United Lutheran Church in America set aside funds for the creation of a television series, culminating in 1960 with the production of the animated program *Davey and Goliath*, which was produced through 1975.[36]

In the same year the United Lutheran Church of America was involved in production, Pat Robertson founded the Christian Broadcasting Network, which now broadcasts around the world. Another broadcast pioneer, David Mainse, founded what is now Crossroads Christian Communications in Canada in 1962. The next year, the Southern Baptist Radio and Television Commission released *Jot the Dot*, an animated series for children, created by Ruth Byers.[37]

The decades of the 70s and 80s were a time of cultural and political change, and yet represented opportunities for experimentation with various media by Creatives. In the 1970s, Russ Doughten and Donald Thompson created Mark IV Pictures, best known for end-time films such as *A Thief in the Night, A Distant Thunder, Image of the Beast*, and *The Prodigal Planet*.[38] Trinity Broadcasting Network was founded in 1973 by Paul Crouch and is now carried on numerous stations worldwide, featuring a wide array of programs for all ages. Between 1981 and 1983, the Christian Broadcasting Network created two animated series, *Superbook* and *The Flying House*. Both aired initially in Japan, and eventually worldwide. It is estimated that nearly 500 million people have viewed *Superbook*.[39] *Superbook* is now being redesigned using 3D animation technology.

> ***Veggie Tales* has been an extremely successful series in Christian and commercial markets.**

Big Idea was founded by Phil Vischer in 1989. Vischer and Mike Nawrocki broke new ground by incorporating 3D animation technology and "talking vegetables" to convey Biblical stories and morals. *Veggie Tales* has been an extremely successful series in Christian and commercial markets. *Adventures in Odyssey, Hermie and Friends*, and *McGee and Me* have also been highly successful series developed for children. As the new millennium drew closer, interest in end-time events grew in popularity. In 1995, Paul Lalonde cofounded Cloud Ten Pictures, and began producing the *Left Behind* series in 2000.[40] By the beginning of the new millennium, churches were involved in movie making. For example, Sherwood Pictures, one of the ministries of Albany, Georgia based Sherwood Baptist Church, created *Flywheel* (2003), *Facing the Giants* (2006), *Fireproof* (2008), and *Courageous* (2011).[41] In 2011 Roma Downey, best known for her role in the *Touched by an Angel* television series, and her husband Mark Burnett, producer of television shows, including *Survivor* and *The Apprentice*, created LightWorkers Media. By 2013, *The Bible* miniseries was broadcast on the History Channel. The production is the recipient of three Emmy Award nominations, and has had over 100 million viewers. Burnett and Downey went on to release *Son of God* as a major motion picture in 2014, adapted from the successful miniseries.[42] Kirk Cameron, who acted on the sitcom *Growing Pains*, has also been heavily involved in making faith based movies for some time now.

Computer Compatible

Advances in computer technology after mid-century, particularly personal computing, became a new venue for Christian Creatives. One of the first companies to create computer games with Biblical content was *BibleBytes*, founded in 1982 by John Joyce and Phillip Conrod. Games were created for use on such platforms as Apple IIe, Applesoft BASIC, Commodore BASIC, Commodore 64, Commodore VIC-20, and Visual Basic. Among game titles were *Bible Scrabble Games, The Memory Verse Games, The Quail Game* and *Moses' Rod*.[43]

In the late 80s, Arizona based Wisdom Tree Incorporated was created and began focusing on media for both entertainment and education. During the 90s, the company developed Bible games with titles such as *Bible Adventures, Bible Man, Exodus, GodSpeed, Heaven Bound*, and *Interactive Parables*.[44] By 2000, N'Lightning Software Development Incorporated released one of the first 3D shooter action games, *Catechumen*, with a story arc based in Rome during the time of Christian persecution. Based on the *Left Behind* book series by Tim LaHaye, the video game *Left Behind:Eternal Forces* was created in 2006, followed by other titles.

Denominations are also capitalizing on the vast potential of the Internet. While its initial development grew from government and military applications, church and para-church ministries today utilize it for evangelism, education, and entertainment. Gone are the days when the major means of communication with constituents was the printed Sunday morning bulletin.

Today, specifically designed interfaces for video and audio streaming, blogs, podcasts, and social media provide opportunities for interaction and access at any time. There are also churches that are fully online, meeting in chat rooms or as avatars in virtual reality environments. Virtual churches can be configured to include text-based clickable links representing rooms in a church, with "rooms" that include an entrance, youth room, sanctuary, music room, gallery, library, fellowship hall, or kitchen.

Pioneer Creative Catalyst's Story

Sandra Bowden,
Past President, Christians in the Visual Arts
Founder, The Bowden Collections

Sandra Bowden has dedicated her career to helping church rediscover its rich visual heritage and embrace the visual arts and its artists again. She is first an artist, but also a collector of art relating to the Bible and curator of exhibitions. Bowden says, "When I consider the long history of Christian art I am reminded that these people left a record that faith was alive and well in their time, and I hope that my art will leave such an evidence of faith to add to that legacy."

Bowden's art is a record of her spiritual and intellectual journey. From the early 1970s the biblical text itself has dominated her iconography. Wayne Rosa wrote in *The Art of Sandra Bowden* that *"Exploring the role of language in Sandra Bowden's art is a bit like exploring the role of DNA in human biology and personality…language is a generative force in her art."* Bowden has said that she marvels at how a small group of symbols, called letters, can be used to suggest sound, form words, fill books, carry meaning and allow us to communicate with one another, even across the barriers of time and place. And most amazing of all is that God has chosen to communicate with us through language.

Her art uses language in two ways; both structurally in its visual character using the alphabet, signs and symbols of language, and as the subject of her art whereby she explores the great gift and mystery of language over the history of humankind with special focus to how it has related to the Bible, Judaism and Christianity.

For over forty years a signature element of her work has been the inclusion of a Hebrew text, compacted by eliminating spaces between words and line, carefully inscribed, but not intended to be read. The theme or title of each piece usually finds it source from the passage. It is essential for her that the Scripture be accurately present, however, it is not important to decipher the words. The textural impact of these sections invites the viewer to draw near and examine the surface. In the mid-1990s she began gilding these text panels to add another veil and enhance the richness of the surface.

Another device used to covey a conversation over time is the layering of one text upon another resembling medieval palimpsests, parchment sheets where erased texts bleed through the surface. Her collages often begin by laying down a page from an old Bible or musical facsimile, then added layers of thin Japanese papers veil the text beneath the surface. To further enhance this visual exchange she many times adds a handwritten script from another source. By the time the section is finished it is nearly impossible to readily decipher any of the inscriptions. Bowden is interested in that fleeting moment when we catch a glimpse of the truth, or momentarily grasp an association. This glimpse is enough to open the conversation, if we are willing to be sensitive and attentive.

She writes, "I came out of tradition in which the Word was central. God's Word was the Bible and clear answers to all of life's questions could be found in these words. I am thankful for the rich tradition of Bible study and encouragement to know and reverence God's Word. But I sensed there was more to the picture than definitive theological understandings.

My spiritual journey has awakened me to the power of mystery, a place where all is not fully understood and we are privileged to only a glimpse of the truth. As I studied Hebrew and archaeology to personally mine the scriptures more profoundly, I came to see that the Word was not just written in a book, but that Christ was the Word. Here lies the mystery of the gospel. "In the beginning was the word, the word was with God and the word was God...the word became flesh and dwelt among us." This epiphany brought my work full circle, connecting the Word with the Image of the unseen God."

Her most recent works use actual books that have been screwed open and finished to display a variety of surfaces which include the familiar raised Hebrew and Greek texts, Braille, or graphic elements carefully incised onto the luminescent painted books. Sandra Bowden writes, "The fascination of the book as the vehicle for my art and a container for the *Word* has only grown over the years, and points my compass to the future."

She has had over one hundred solo shows including the Bible Lands Museum in Jerusalem, Haifa Museum in Israel, Patmos Gallery, Toronto, Canada, Foxhall Gallery in Washington DC, and Gordon College in Wenham, Massachusetts. Her work has been in numerous invitational shows and juried exhibitions all across the United States and internationally. Featured articles on her work have been found in Christianity Today and Christianity and the Arts, as well as the Chicago Tribune, Albany Times Union, E. Gene Vieth's book *State of the Arts: From Bezalel to Maplethorpe* and in *It Was Good: Making Art to the Glory of God*. In 2005 Square Halo Books published a 200 page full-color book on her work, *The Art of Sandra Bowden*.

In 1980 she made a deliberate choice to work only in the field of Christianity and art— decision that has freed her to spend time in several volunteer positions making a significant contribution to the field. For fourteen years Sandra was president of Christians in the Visual Arts, a national organization dedicated to exploring and nurturing the relationship of the visual arts and the Christian faith. As a founding member she has served as Vice Chairman on the board of the Museum of Biblical Art in New York City.

She has curated several exhibitions for Christians in Visual Arts which includes Beauty Given by Grace: The Biblical Prints of sadao Watanabe and Seeing the Savior: Images from the Life of Jesus. She is also a passionate collector of religious art with work from the early fifteenth century to the present time. As a way to help the church become familiar with its rich treasure of art, she offers from her personal collection, known as Bowden Collections, several exhibitions that travel to churches, universities, seminaries and museums. Some of these include: *Seeing Christ in the Darkness: Georges Rouault* as Graphic Artist; Marc Chagall and the Bible; Otto Dix Matthaüs Evangelium; Most Highly Favored: The Life of the Virgin Mary and many others which can be found on www.bowdencollections.com.

Sandra Bowden concentrated on biblical studies at Berkshire Christian College, and then studied art at the Massachusetts College of Art in Boston. In 1978 she graduated with a degree in art from SUNY at Empire State College. She has studied biblical archaeology, ancient and modern Hebrew and geology as a way to enrich her painting and printmaking.

Pioneer Creative Catalyst's Story

Makoto Fujimura,
Founder, International Arts Movement (IAM) and Fujimura Institute

Makoto Fujimura recipient of his fourth honorary doctorate, (Roanoke College, May 2015), is an artist, writer, and speaker who is recognized worldwide as a cultural shaper. A Presidential appointee to the National Council on the Arts from 2003-2009, Fujimura served as an international advocate for the arts, speaking with decision makers and advising governmental policies on the arts. In 2014, the American Academy of Religion, named Makoto Fujimura as its '2014 Religion and the Arts' award recipient. This award is presented annually to an artist, performer, critic, curator, or scholar who has made a significant contribution to the understanding of the relations among the arts and the religions, both for the academy and for a broader public. Previous recipients of the award include Meredith Monk, Holland Carter, Gary Snyder, Betye & Alison Saar and Bill Viola.

Fujimura's work is exhibited at galleries around the world, including Dillon Gallery in New York, Sato Museum in Tokyo, The Contemporary Museum of Tokyo, Tokyo National University of Fine Arts Museum, Bentley Gallery in Arizona, Gallery Exit and Oxford House at Taikoo Place in Hong Kong, and Vienna's Belvedere Museum. He is one of the first artists to paint live on stage at New York City's legendary Carnegie Hall as part of an ongoing collaboration with composer and percussionist Susie Ibarra.

A popular speaker, he has lectured at numerous conferences, universities and museums, including the Aspen Institute, Yale and Princeton Universities, Sato Museum and the Phoenix Art Museum. Fujimura founded the International Arts Movement in 1992, a non-profit whose "Encounter" conferences have featured cultural catalysts such as Dr. Elaine Scarry, Dennis Donoghue, Billy Collins, Dana Gioia, Calvin DeWitt and Miroslav Volf.

Fujimura's second book, *Refractions: A Journey of Faith, Art and Culture*, is a collection of essays bringing together people of all backgrounds in a conversation and meditation on culture, art, and humanity. In celebration of the 400th Anniversary of the King James Bible, Crossway Publishing commissioned and published The Four Holy Gospels, featuring Fujimura's illuminations of the sacred texts. In December 2014, his latest book, 'Culture Care' was launched and has experienced asignificant global response.

In 2011 the Fujimura Institute was established and launched the Four Qu4rtets, a collaboration between Fujimura, painter Bruce Herman, Duke theologian/pianist Jeremy Begbie, and Yale composer Christopher Theofanidis, based on T.S. Eliot's Four Quartets. The exhibition will travel to Baylor, Duke, and Yale Universities, Gordon College and other institutions around the globe.

Bucknell University honored him with the Outstanding Alumni Award in 2012.

He is a recipient of three Doctor of Arts Honorary Degrees, from Belhaven University in 2011, Biola University in 2012 and Cairn University earlier this year.

SIX

Dance

Since the 1990s, the International Christian Dance Fellowship has grown to include members in Australia, Britain, Canada, Costa Rica, Fiji, France, Germany, Ghana, Holland, Hong Kong, India (South), Indonesia, Ireland, Italy, Jamaica, Kenya, Korea, Malaysia, Puerto Rico, Singapore, South Africa, St Maarten, Suriname, Sweden, Trinidad and Tobago, and America.

Church of the
Transfiguration, 1936
St. Mark's-in-the-Bouwerie,
New York, New York
Courtesy of Library of Congress

Nineteenth century holiness camp meetings were noted for evangelical preaching and exuberant worship. Physical characteristics included falling out in the Spirit, laughter, and "dancing in the Spirit" which carried over to the Pentecostal movement at the dawn of the twentieth century. Yet at the beginning of the twentieth century, dance was considered anathema in the majority of American churches. United Methodist, Baptist, and Presbyterian churches, for example, had doctrinal stances that forbade such activities.

Turn of the Century Dance
One of the first forays into dance took place at Saint Mark Episcopal Church in New York City.

The rector of the church, William Guthrie, began including liturgical dance somewhere around 1920 during services. In the 1930s, the liturgical dance group was involved in the Chautauqua circuit under the direction of Guthrie's daughter Phoebe.[1]

Dance continued to be part of the churches of the traditional Pentecostal movement to mid-century. Because these churches grew out of the holiness movement, strictures against dancing carried over as well. Distinguishing factors; however, allowed for this expression as the individual was so led or "filled by the Holy Spirit" that physical exuberance was manifested. This type of dance was not necessarily learned, but tended to be spontaneous in nature and meant to express worship to God with the whole being–body, mind, and spirit.

Renewal

By the early 1960s, two renewal movements occurred that would be instrumental in making dance an accepted expression of worship for larger segments of Christianity: the Charismatic and Jesus movements. Each crossed denominational lines inside and outside traditional Pentecostal circles and included the arts in worship. Dance, both spontaneous and planned, was one of the most visible of the expressions and often accompanied the music of each movement. For example, the Shekinah Dance Troupe, one of the earliest ministries of its type, developed dance routines for religious purposes.[2]

Toymaker & Son

Colin Harbinson's internationally successful Toymaker & Son was first performed in England in 1978 at Chesworth Middle School in Horsham, where he served as acting Headmaster. From there, it moved on to Italy, Western Europe, and Greece. In 1980, Toymaker & Son was performed for the 1980 Winter Olympics in Lake Placid, then again for the Summer Olympics, held in 1984 in Los Angeles. Toymaker & Son was sponsored as part of the World Cup Soccer Games held in Spain in 1982. In that same year, it was performed as part of the Commonwealth Games in Australia. Toymaker & Son has been seen by millions of people in 60 nations, both in person and through media. This groundbreaking production was one of the first of its type and helped open the door for the integration of multiple art forms (especially dance and theatre) in churches around the world.[3]

The 1980s brought the development of professional para-church dance organizations offering an array of dance classes and performances, as well as outreach internationally. It was also a time when dance and ballet continued to be included in churches from various denominations.

Ballet Magnificat!

In 1986, Kathy Thibodeaux founded Ballet Magnificat! in Jackson, Mississippi. Both she and her husband Keith Thibodeaux brought extensive professional artistic experience at the outset of the new organization. Keith Thibodeaux became the Executive Director of Ballet Magnificat! in 1993. Thibodeaux has an extensive background in television, as well as a songwriter, singer, drummer and a member of the pioneering Christian rock band *David and the Giants*.[3]

> **In 1989, Ballet Magnificat! opened the School of the Arts with the purpose of training dancers, ages three to adult, "in excellence to use their gifts and talents to glorify the Lord Jesus Christ."**

Kathy Thibodeaux was one of the first dancers under contract with what was then Jackson Ballet Company, now known as Ballet Mississippi. She appeared in performances such as *The Nutcracker, Graduation Ball, Swan Lake, Pas de Quatre, Don Quixote, Le Corsaire,* and *Raymonda*. On the international level, Kathy Thibodeaux was awarded the silver medal at the USA International Ballet Competition in 1982. At the time of the founding of Ballet Magnificat!, Thibodeaux had achieved the level of Principal Dancer. In 2008, she was the recipient of the Hartley D. Peavey Award for Entrepreneurial Excellence. Her work at Ballet Magnificat! has been multifaceted, and has included directing, performance, and choreography.[4]

In 1989, Ballet Magnificat! opened the School of the Arts with the purpose of training dancers, ages three to adult, "in excellence to use their gifts and talents to glorify the Lord Jesus Christ."[5] Classes are offered to some 400 students in areas such as creative movement, ballet vocabulary, and terminology, through the Vagonova ballet method.[6] Summer Dance Intensives

Worship Dancers performing
© Kristy-Anne Glubish/Design Pics/Corbis

and Teacher Intensives are offered annually to students from the United States and abroad and include classes in ballet, pointe, pas de deux, modern conditioning, and improvisation. Ballet Magnificat!'s touring companies have ministered extensively for many years state side and internationally in churches and various venues.[7]

Christian Dance Fellowship

As the decade of the 90s opened, movements internationally helped shape the creation of a new dance organization for Creatives in America. Beginning in 1991, preparations were made for a national Christian dance conference and organization. The Christian Dance Fellowship of America (CDFA) ultimately became a reality in 1992 at the Movement Arts in Worship Conference, with Pamela Hall as first National Coordinator. The CDFA was an outgrowth of a multination Christian dance movement, ultimately culminating in the International Christian Dance Fellowship, which was established in 1988 in Australia by pioneering dance artist Mary Jones. Jones had established the Christian Dance Fellowship of Australia in 1978 and by 1987 had a vision for an international organization for Christian dancers.[8] Since the 1990s, the International Christian Dance Fellowship has grown to include members in Australia, Britain, Canada, Costa Rica, Fiji, France, Germany, Ghana, Holland, Hong Kong, India (South), Indonesia, Ireland, Italy, Jamaica, Kenya, Korea, Malaysia, Puerto Rico, Singapore, South Africa, St Maarten, Suriname, Sweden, Trinidad and Tobago, and America.[9]

Crossings Dance

After founding the Christian Dance Fellowship of Canada in 1990, Karen Sudds founded Crossings Dance Ministries in 1992, Canada's first company offering liturgical dance skills. Sudds trained at the University of Calgary, as well as liturgical dance studies in Singapore and Australia. As the CDM grew, Sudds decided to offer professional performance opportunities for the student population by creating Corps Bara Dance Guild and Corps Bara Dance Theatre. Program offerings include Classical Ballet, Preschool Ballet, Modern/Contemporary, Jazz/Modern Fusion, Tap, Hip Hop/ Urban and Musical Theatre.[10]

Masterworks Touring Company

Anora Hummel's career in dance began at mid-century and has influenced hundreds of dancers since that time. Prior to relocation to Virginia in the 80s, Hummel owned Anora's Studio of Dance, located across the country in Arizona, where nearly 600 students took Ballet, Tap, and Jazz lessons. In 1989, Hummel developed another dance business, Academie de Ballet, which has since grown to be one of the largest dance studios on the East Coast, with over 650 students and four studios. In 1991, Hummel founded Masterworks Touring Company, located in Chesapeake Virginia. With the slogan "We have been called to dance with passion unto the glory of God," Masterworks Touring Company's mission is to "present the Good News of Jesus

> **Masterworks Touring Company's mission is to "present the Good News of Jesus Christ through dance, drama and personal testimonies."**

Christ through dance, drama and personal testimonies. We long to see the Lord redeem and restore the arts for His good purposes."[11]

National Liturgical Dance Network

Founded in 1998 by Eyesha Marable, the National Liturgical Dance Network's mission is to train leaders for churches and liturgical organizations.[12] The organization consists of over 35 member groups nationally and internationally and offers classes in liturgical dance. In order to implement their creative goals, the organization strives to use dance a means of witness, edify the church, promote an intimate relationship with God, and provide training for dance ministries.[13]

Ad Deum

Ad Deum Dance Company was founded in 2000 by Randall Flinn in Houston, Texas, as a professional Christian modern dance organization. Flinn's experience spans 25 years, including work in America and internationally, working with organizations such as Cirque Du Soleil-Alegria, Ballet Magnificat!, Belhaven University, Project Dance New York, Los Angeles, Sydney, Australia, as well as organizations in Europe and Asia.[14] Ad Deum's mission is to "create and perform excellent and vital works of dance that serve to wash over the heart and soul of humanity with relevant meaning and redemptive hope."[15] Classes are offered in Modern/Contemporary, Ballet, and Jazz. Ad Deum also offers both spring and summer dance intensives, as well as specialized workshops.[16] Today, Ad Deum is made up of 27 dancers led by Randall Flinn and comprised of two divisions, the Main Company and Ad Deum 2.

Jubilate School of the Arts

With roots going back to 1988, Jubilate School of Art began when the founder, Domini Boling, offered dance classes in North Carolina. Today, Jubilate School of Art offers Certificates in Worship Dance Choreography. Examples of courses offered include Worship Choreography Technique and Biblical Dance, Understanding the Use of Music in Worship Choreography, Group and Solo Choreography. The organization also hosts Jubilate Worship Dance Conferences and in 2014 began the Jubilate International School of Choreography & Worship Dance.[17]

Project Dance

With initial beginnings dating back to 1996, New York based Project Dance was founded in 2002 by Cheryl Cutlip, who has had an extensive career as a professional dancer. Her resume includes 15 years as a Radio City Rockette, serving as captain, assistant choreographer, and national spokesperson, including interviews with Katie Couric, Diane Sawyer, and Larry King. Cutlip has also danced in the Broadway National Tour CRAZY FOR YOU and WALKERDANCE Company (under the direction of Chet Walker). Project Dance serves approximately 1,500 dancers worldwide and has performed in cities such as New York, London, Sydney, Hong Kong and Washington DC. A unique feature of the group is that many of their dances are performed in the open air, making them more accessible to the public. The Project Dance foundation also has two other programs, Broadway Underground and Atmosphere, the former providing a platform to showcase new talent, the latter offering fellowship opportunities to dancers in New York City. Master classes are offered and include instructors from Broadway, The Radio City Rockettes, Alvin Ailey American Dance Theater, Martha Graham Dance Company, and So You Think You Can Dance.[18]

Word in Motion

Although Word in Motion was officially founded in 2004, the dance company had gone through several prior versions. The founders, Tymme and Aury Reitz,

Harlem Hip Hop Church
© Alex Masi/Corbis

had danced for artists such as Madonna, Will Smith, Missy Elliott, Backstreet Boys, and others before going into ministry. According to the Word in Motion website, their "work has been highlighted in annual award shows, network television, films, commercials, and stage productions."[17]

After coming to the Lord, they ministered and performed in various capacities until founding The Arts Prophetically Speaking Dance Ministry in 2001. In 2004, the Reitz's created Word In Motion Dance Company to continue the stated mission of developing a nation of dancers for Christ. Since 2005, they have worked with "The Underground" ministry service which integrates a variety of arts including Hip Hop, Contemporary Music, and released their debut album, "On Fire" in 2010.

Expressions of Joy

Florida based Expressions of Joy was founded in 2005 by Josi Geyer and Tom Walker, with a mission to "nurture artists to their highest potential for outreach through original and innovative Christ-centered performances."[18] Lessons are taught using Classical Ballet as a foundation. Other classes include Modern and Contemporary dance. Radiant Dance Company is Expressions of Joy's student dance company and holds performances in venues such as the community and churches.[19]

Dancelink

Dancelink is a ministry of OMArts International under the direction of Linda Wells, who was a professional dancer in England. The ministry has performed in numerous locations around the world in including Italy, Hungary, Birmingham, UK, Azerbaijan, Albania, and Turkey. The goal of Dancelink is "to send and train dancers of all levels to use their gifts to worship and minister on the mission field." Opportunities for missions have included Transform 2013: Dancelink/OMArts International France and Transform 2013: Dancelink/OMArts International Malta. In 2013 alone, 56 dancers were sent out in short-term missions opportunities through Dancelink.[22]

Paradosi Ballet Company

Joel and Tennille Carver founded Paradosi Ballet Company in 2007, which, according to the company website, is the first professional Christian dance company in the Pacific Northwest. The company's goal is to "share Christ through dance, drama and personal witness." In 2009, Surrendered School of the Arts was created to offer classes such as Ballet, Jazz, Hip Hop, Tap, Drama, Piano, Guitar, Voice, Zumba, and Art. The company now has campuses in Tacoma, Auburn, and Orting Washington.[23]

Ballet 5:8

Ballet 5:8 was also created in 2009, the culmination of efforts by Julianna Slager, who now serves as Artistic Director, and Amy Kozol Sanderson, Executive Director.

The company offers several formats to attain skills, including trainee and summer programs and the School of the Arts. The trainee program provides learning opportunities for students seeking a career in dance performance. summer programs include intensives, workshops, and children's camps. Skills learned through Ballet 5:8 include areas such as ballet, pointe, variations, partnering, repertoire, modern, contemporary, and conditioning. The School of the Arts provides professional training in three divisions: preprofessional, children, and adult.[24] And while it is true that many Christian institutions of higher learning offer undergraduate degrees in the arts, opportunities for graduate level work have been scarce. However, a growing movement in higher education has taken place over the last quarter century to provide opportunities for research in theology, philosophy, and the arts.

Pioneer Creative Catalyst's Story

Keith and Kathy Thibodeaux,
Founders of Ballet Magnificat!

Ballet Magnificat! is really a miracle birthed by the Spirit of God. The name actually means the "ballet that magnifies the Lord" (Luke 1:46). Through much prayer and waiting on the right timing Ballet Magnificat! began in 1986. Pastors, and men and women of God spoke many encouraging words as we undertook what was a pioneering work of likeminded dancers. We believed God wanted us to use our talents for His Kingdom and for His good news. As a principle dancer in Ballet Mississippi, the idea of Kathy beginning a "Christian ballet" seemed like the most ridiculous thing she could think of. Kathy won the silver medal in the 1982 USA International Ballet Competition and had offers from New York and other places to dance, but chose not to. The president of Belhaven University in our hometown of Jackson, Mississippi, saw an article in the paper about Kathy's step of faith. He offered to help us by offering studio space, an office, and use of a computer. Little by little, Christian dancers from other companies heard about Ballet Magnificat! and moved to Jackson. Even though most of them knew there was no guarantee of security and finances, they chose to step out in faith with us.

Opportunities to dance came after we sent letters and flyers to churches describing our company. Love offerings from these events were distributed within the company according to financial need. At times, some of the dancers used their own credit cards to help with financial needs, such a blown out tire. Kathy's dad would sometimes help by paying for gas and with other needs. This crazy idea, by the world's standards, would be accepted by more and more churches, and touring began to take up most of the year. We established the School of the Arts shortly afterwards. Parents of children in Jackson loved the idea of excellent ballet training taught in a Christian atmosphere.

In the beginning there were doubters who said we would never get support and funding. There were others in churches that thought dance was inappropriate. God took care of our finances because everyone in the company was in submission to God's will. We weren't afraid to sacrifice–to set up lights, flooring, or sound–and then dance to see the vision come to reality. Once churches saw that our costumes were modest and tasteful, and our choreography was paired with a true heart of worship, their doubts of inappropriateness vanished.

Today, Ballet Magnificat is comprised of two professional touring companies that travel across America and Internationally. The School of the Arts has 300 students, as well as 40 others from around the world who live here and work in our trainee program. Our summer workshops, which last two to four weeks, attract 300-400 dancers each year. What began as a dream and a vision for Kathy and me has grown so much more than we could have ever imagined. Now there are numerous Christian dance companies and Christian school in the United States. Belhaven University has a successful dance program that began with Ballet Magnificat's idea and training resources. We are just amazed at all God has accomplished. We look forward to growing in the grace and knowledge of our Savior Jesus. As we knock on doors and seek after Him, He will open other doors for us to walk through.

SEVEN

Intersections: Theology, Education, Arts

> "The conversation between theology and the arts at an academic level has burgeoned in the last two or three decades. Thirty years ago, the resources were relatively limited. Today, especially in the UK and North America, but also further afield, we are witnessing a growing interest in the interface between sustained theological thinking on the one hand, and artistic practices and theory on the other."
>
> —INSTITUTE FOR THEOLOGY, IMAGINATION AND THE ARTS
> UNIVERSITY OF ST. ANDREWS, SCOTLAND

Duke University Chapel,
Durham, North Carolina
© Paul Souders/Corbis

Jeremy Begbie's work with the Initiative in Theology and the Arts represents a growing trend to offer educational opportunities for those interested in the intersection of theology, the arts, and practice. A number of degrees have been developed to meet the growing educational demand in the field of theology and the arts. Opportunities for research in the areas of aesthetics, philosophy, liturgical arts, dance, music, visual art, theater, and architecture, from a uniquely theological view, have increased and reflect the growth of the movement.

Duke Divinity School

In 2008, Jeremy Begbie established the Institute for Theology, Imagination and the Arts at Duke Divinity School. Prior to his work at Duke, Begbie was director of Theology through the Arts housed in the Institute for Theology, Imagination, and the Arts at the University of St. Andrews, Scotland. He is also a senior member at Wolfson College, Cambridge. The aim of the Institute is to "demonstrate what theology can contribute to the arts and what the arts can contribute to society" with the purpose of "contributing towards transformative leadership in the Church, academy and society and enriching theological education in the academy and society."[1]

A variety of strategies are used to accomplish these goals. The program offers the Doctor of Theology degree with a concentration in the arts. A number of courses and distinguished lectures are offered. Research colloquia are presented in Theology and Music, Theology and the Built Environment, and The Arts and Theology in Modernity. Events such as exhibits, concerts, readings, lectures, and performances promote interfaces with the arts.[2]

Dominican School of Philosophy and Theology

Dominican School of Philosophy and Theology's Master of Theological Studies offers four areas of study–Christian Ethics, Catholic Social Teaching, Thomistic Studies, and Religion and the Arts. The Religion and the Arts program requirements include study in the areas of philosophy and theology, studio, thesis, and language. Among the many courses offered include Old Testament Foundations, the Bible in the Arts, Christian Iconography, and Philosophical Aesthetics. A study abroad opportunity is provided in Rome at the Angelicum, University of St. Thomas Aquinas. Among possible courses offered are Liturgical Theology and Practice, Sacred Art, and Sacred Architecture. Blackfriars Gallery is located on campus and is used for performances and exhibits.[3]

Fuller Theological Seminary

Through the School of Theology at Fuller Theological Seminary, students may earn a Certificate in Theology and the Arts, Master of Divinity, Master of Theology or Master of Arts in Theology, and Ministry with emphasis in either Theology and the Arts or Worship, Theology and the Arts, and a Doctorate of Philosophy in Theology, Art, Culture, and Worship. The School of Theology works closely with The Brehm Center for Worship, Theology, and the Arts, which has developed initiatives in diverse areas related to music, visual faith, an institute for art and architecture, film, worship, preaching, and culture. The Center's emphasis states:

Through the offering of Fuller Theological Seminary, the center empowers and equips a new generation of artists and church leaders to effectively integrate worship, theology, and the arts in order to enrich the encounter with God and the world.[4]

Graduate Theological Union

Offering both Master of Arts and Doctor of Philosophy degrees in Art and Religion, the Graduate Theological Union offers students research opportunities for a wide range of topics in arts such as visual arts, film, dance, drama, literature, and music, as well as history, philosophy, aesthetics, and theology. As part of a consortium, students may take courses from a number of institutions.[5]

Regent College

Located in Vancouver, Regent College's Master of Arts in Theological Studies and Master of Divinity degrees offer concentrations in Christianity, Church, and Culture, with focused studies in Christianity and the Arts. Among the courses offered are The Christian Imagination, Vocation of the Artist, seminars, integrative projects, and electives. Other courses are taken in Old Testament, New Testament, Biblical Languages, History of Christianity, and Christian Thought and Culture.[6] Located on the campus of the University of British Columbia, regarding the place of the arts on campus, the College states "[t]he arts play a central role at Regent College, and we pay great attention to the physical space in which we study, work, and interact."[7] In 1990, The Lookout Gallery was created to "demonstrate the significance and centrality of the visual arts" and has displayed work in a variety of media around the world including drawings, prints, and sculpture.[8]

University of St. Andrews, Scotland

The Institute for Theology, Imagination and the Arts was established in 2000 from two projects in the School of Divinity at Saint Mary's College. One project, "Theology and Imagination" was led by Trevor Hart, the other, "Theology through the Arts" was led by Jeremy Begbie. Two degrees are offered, the Master of Letters in Theology, Imagination, and the Arts and the Doctor of Theology in Theology, Imagination, and the Arts. The Master's degree offers modules such as Theological Engagements with the Arts, A Christian Doctrine of the Arts and Religious Experience and Aesthetic Theory. The Doctoral student works under the consultation of a supervisor, who helps refine research interests. Seminars, conferences, and colloquia related to the arts and culture are presented on a regular basis.[9]

Yale University Divinity School and Institute of Sacred Music

Yale University's Institute of Sacred Music and Divinity School offers interdisciplinary research in theology and the arts. The Institute of Sacred Music states that it "engages musicians, artists, clergy, and scholars from around the world in rigorous training and collaboration, and offers a full calendar of concerts, lectures, exhibitions, and other events."[10] Programs in Religion and the Arts include Religion and Literature, Religion and Music, and Religion and Visual Arts. Courses in Religion and Literature include Dante's Journey to God, Religious Themes in Contemporary American Short Fiction, the Psalms in Scripture, Literature, and Music, and The Religious Lyric in Britain. The Religion and Music program also works with the School of Music and Department of Music at Yale, and is open to students interested in historical musicology or ethnomusicology. Students interested in pursuing the Religion and Visual Arts concentration have study opportunities in visual and material arts in relation to culture.[11]

Southern Baptist Theological Seminary

Southern Baptist Theological Seminary offers the Doctor of Philosophy degree in Christianity and the Arts in a flexible format in which students take modules twice a year on campus. Research and online interaction is conducted in preparation for on-campus course work. Once comprehensive exams are completed, students conduct research to prepare for the dissertation defense.

The degree is intended to offer "biblical, historical and contemporary perspective to engage with the visual arts, literature and film."[12] A variety of courses are offered in aesthetic theology and Christianity in relation to visual arts, film, performing arts and music.[13]

Wesley Theological Seminary

The purpose of the Master of Arts in Theology and the Arts at Wesley Theological Seminary is "[t]o provide a general theological degree blended with a certificate in the practice of arts ministry."[14] Courses in Hebrew Bible, New Testament, Church History, and Systematic Theology are foundational to the degree. Arts Ministry coursework requires study in theory, various arts disciplines, and a focus on one art discipline.[15] An Arts and Theology track is offered in Wesley's Doctor of Ministry degree.

The Henry Luce Center for the Arts and Religion plays an important role in the intersection of the arts and theology at Wesley. Through the Center, a number of events such as dramas, concerts, talks, poetry readings, dance, workshops, exhibits (through the Dadian Gallery) artist-in-residencies, and symposia are presented.[16]

By the beginning of twenty-first century, a number of institutions were offering degrees providing opportunities for research on the intersection of the arts and theology. These degrees allowed educators, laity, artists, ministers, and leaders from a wide array of denominations to research the expanding field. Many of the degrees emphasized the integration of the arts in churches in practical ways. Denominations across the country integrated arts to influence the local church, community, and culture.

> **Arts Ministry coursework requires study in theory, various arts disciplines, and a focus on one art discipline.**

EIGHT

A Snapshot:
Congregations, Denominations, and the Arts

> Using the talents God gave us, we are able to share the Gospel in worship and outreach. We invite you to participate in our Fine Arts Ministries program as we seek to glorify God through music, drama, dance and the visual arts.
> —FIRST PRESBYTERIAN CHURCH
> LAKELAND, FLORIDA

Outdoor reenactments have been a growing trend as congregational expressions of worship.
© depositphoto/DesignPicsInc

Fine Arts Department

A growing trend has developed on the local and denominational level to integrate the arts in the life of the Church. Dance, music, dinner theatre, orchestra, fine arts series, arts academies and schools, talent competitions, outdoor reenactments, visual arts, and art galleries have emerged as congregational expressions of worship. Whereas vocational titles for church workers have traditionally included Senior Pastor, Associate Pastor, Minister of Christian Education, and Minister of Music, new titles such as Minister of Fine Arts, Worship Arts Pastor, Creative Arts Pastor, Arts Director, Technical Arts Director, and Graphic Designer are now included. Denominations have departments focused on the arts on a national level and also provide college and university professional preparation in the arts. Some congregations, such as Hillsong Church in Australia, are deeply involved in the arts and have multisite locations in other nations. From a uniquely Christian worldview, the arts play an ever-increasing role in churches on a local, national and international level. The following is a snapshot of various facets of the movement within churches on a local and national level.

Fine Arts Academies and Schools

The Columbia Institute of Fine Arts. Columbia Baptist Church, located in Falls Church, Virginia, established the Columbia Institute of Fine Arts in 1993 "to provide quality instruction in the arts and to help prepare students for future service through the development of skills for performance and ministry."[1] The Institute functions as an outreach of the Worship, Music, and Arts Ministry of the church, with faculty offering a wide array of skills and experience, including musical instruments, ballet, dance, and group performance.

Private lessons are offered in ballet and tap, cello, euphonium, flute, French horn, guitar, handbells, harp, organ, piano, saxophone, trombone, trumpet, tuba, viola, violin, and voice. A course designed for volunteer choir members is offered to provide basic skills in areas such as voice, breath management, pitch, diction, and interpretation. A chamber music ensemble course is available to those who wish to gain skills in playing in a group.[2] The Institute also maintains a School of Dance, MusikGarten early childhood music education program, Rock &Roll class for intermediate and high school students, and Abrakadoodle Art program art education curriculum.[3]

> From a uniquely Christian worldview, the arts play an ever-increasing role in churches on a local and national and international level.

St. Luke's United Methodist Church School of the Arts. Established in 1994, Saint Luke's United Methodist Church School of the Arts offers educational opportunities in a variety of arts including music, visual art, dance, and drama. The reason for the Academy, as stated by the church, is to "cultivate spirituality through the arts" through God-given talents and abilities.[4] One of the goals of the church is to create an atmosphere for exploration of the arts that will act as an outreach to the community. This is accomplished through experienced Christian instructors who have notable achievements in the field.[5] An array of classes is offered in string, wind, percussion, dance, photography, painting, and after-school instruction.[6] Faculty has degrees from the Southeastern University, Northwestern State University, Point Park University, Stetson University, University of Central Florida, Montclair State College, and Florida State University among others.[7]

Carmel Lutheran Church Fine Arts Academy. Carmel Lutheran Church in Carmel, Indiana, offers a 1-week summer camp with courses in visual and performing arts for primary (ages Kindergarten through first grade), intermediate (second through fourth grade), and junior high (fifth through eighth grade) school students. Primary students take classes in movement, choir, handchimes, and art. Intermediate and junior high students pick three elective courses and two alternate courses from a wide range of arts courses including cartooning, clothing embellishment, creative writing/bookmaking, dance/hip hop, dance/lyrical, drama/reader's theater, drawing, handbells, jewelry with quilling, mime, mixed media collage, needlework, painting, plaster sculpture, printmaking, radio theater, weaving, and woodworking. The camp at Carmel Lutheran is meant to be a place "where faith, community, and creativity combine in order to praise and glorify God."[8]

Church Arts Departments

Bahamas Faith Ministries International Fellowship. Pastored by the late Myles Munroe, this church's Worship Fine Arts Department consists of a number of areas including dance, banner and flag bearers, dramatists, mime artists, musicians, painters, and singers.[9]

New Antioch Church of God in Christ. Located in Los Angeles, California, the church lists numerous departments, one of which is drama and fine arts. An emphasis on creative expression is mentioned as well as various art forms such as liturgical dance, flag and ribbon ministry, step and drill, as well as drama.[10]

St. John Missionary Baptist Church. This Oklahoma City-based churches' fine arts department focuses on the role of arts to "lead the congregation in worship and praise."[11] Drama, music, orchestra, video, visual praise, and special decorations are listed as forms of art.[12]

First Presbyterian Church. The fine arts department at this Lakeland, Florida based church is listed under the broad umbrella of worship and includes a wide range of opportunities for members. The department offers a performing arts series, adult choirs, youth and children's choir, drama ministry, handbells, liturgical dance, and visual arts. A section on the Presbyterian Book of Order regarding arts in worship is included.[13]

> **Children's activities include choir, bells, chimes, and liturgical movement.**

John Wesley United Methodist Church. Music, dance, instrumental, handbells, and drama groups are all art forms used by the music and fine arts department to minister to members of the congregation in Houston, Texas. The department features a variety of opportunities for adults, including chancel choir, men's ensemble, gospel ensemble, and instrumental ensembles. Children's activities include choir, bells, chimes, and liturgical movement. Youth have arts opportunities in youth choir, bells, liturgical movement, drama, and instrumental ensembles.[14]

Journey Church. A ministry of Journey Church in Norman, Oklahoma, Creative Journey is a means of connecting with other artists, discovering serving opportunities related to creative arts, and taking part in learning opportunities. Classes such as audio/video production, lighting and scenic design, music and fine art are offered. These classes are free, and they accept each person regardless of their level of experience, so that they can grow in their creative talents, using them for the building of God's kingdom. As their websites states, 'Your various gifts and talents have been given to you by God for a purpose – so you can reflect and communicate the story of Christ and His love for the world. That is your purpose. That is your calling.'"[15]

Blue Ridge Community Church. Affiliated with Willow Creek Community Church, Blue Ridge Community Church in Forest, Virginia, has serving opportunities in the areas of music, drama, and technical (camera, sound, lighting, video and IT) areas. Creative stage designs, drama, and the use of various video and graphic design elements, as well as talented vocals and instrumentation promote an environment for worship. A Stage Design team builds each stage with the goal of drawing a person towards Christ. As one team member stated, 'You know a stage design is never going to save anybody. But it does create a certain atmosphere. If it creates a place a person wants to return to, a place where they're going to hear the Gospel, that's what we want.'[16]

Church Art Galleries

Glimpses of His Glory Gallery. Johnson Ferry Baptist Church in Marietta, Georgia, hosts a number of shows in its Glimpses of His Glory Gallery. During the 2014 season, seven exhibits will be shown in the gallery, each with the name of one of the fruits of the Spirit–Patience, Faithfulness, Goodness, Peace, Self Control, Love, and Joy.[17]

House of Hope Presbyterian Church Cloister Art Gallery, St. Paul, Minnesota. Since 2010, the gallery has held numerous shows on its website beginning in 2010. A group of eleven people make up the Arts Committee.[18]

Evergreen Art Gallery. The Evergreen Church, located in Burien, Washington, houses The Evergreen Art Gallery, which has exhibited work by regional, national, and internationally known artists.[19]

Goodrich Gallery. The First United Methodist Church of Dallas, Texas, exhibits shows throughout the year. The goal of the gallery is to bring the church new exhibits on a monthly basis.[20] Paintings, sculpture, photography, and mixed media are representative media of exhibiting artists.

The Gallery. University Lutheran Church in Cambridge, Massachusetts. Since 1993, the gallery has exhibited work in a wide variety of media including photography, painting, stained glass, prints, mixed media, and collage.[21]

Plymouth Art Gallery. Plymouth Congregational Church, Wichita, Kansas. The churches art gallery hosts local artist exhibits that run from one to two months.[22]

Atrium Art Gallery. Second Christian Reformed Church, Grand Haven, Michigan. Exhibits at this church are based on a theme and include works in a wide variety of media such as fiber arts, painting, photography, sculpture, and calligraphy.[23]

Grace Centre Gallery. Located in Mills River, North Carolina, Grace Community Church hosts juried and invitational exhibits.[24]

Fine Arts Series
Westminster Presbyterian Church. This Des Moines, Iowa based church presents a number of events throughout the year including art exhibits, musical and instrumental performances, drama, and seasonal concerts.[25]

First United Methodist Church. The Music Fine Arts Series offers the Sarasota, Florida, community opportunities to attend professional arts events. The series runs from December to April each year and have included concerts and performances such as First Church Jazz Trio and Belle Canto, Christmas Concert, Community Carol Sing, the Chroma Quartet, Organ Series, the Curtis Institute of Music, works by Pergolesi and Stetson University Concert Choir.[26]

> **The St. Paul Fine Arts Series concerts have included a wide range of musical styles, such as jazz, organ, Handel's Messiah, Community Chorales, and Patriotic Concerts.**

St. Paul United Church of Christ. Located in Belleville, Illinois, The St. Paul Fine Arts Series concerts have included a wide range of musical styles, such as jazz, organ, Handel's Messiah, Community Chorales, and Patriotic Concerts.[27]

St. Rita Catholic Church. Saint Rita Fine Arts Series presents musical events intended for members of the parish and north Texas community. Artists with local, national, and international standing are part of the series offerings.[28]

Mount Olive Lutheran Church. The Music and Fine Arts Series at this church, located in Minneapolis, Minnesota, includes music, painting, dance, or drama. With activities almost every month of the year, events have included hymn festivals, organ recitals, and the Mount Olive Cantorei and Cantatas by recognized professionals in the field.[29]

At a Glance—Congregations, Denominations, and the Arts

Assemblies of God. The Assemblies of God denomination has approximately 66 million members and affiliates worldwide.[30] The National Music Department provides resources and consulting for members.[31] National Fine Arts Festivals take place each year beginning in September on the district level and culminate at a national event. Thousands of high school students participate in eight divisions made up of 66 categories. Divisions include art, communication, dance, drama, exhibition, instrumental, vocal, and writing.[32] Evangel College offers Bachelor's degrees among which are Visual Arts, Theatre,

Praise and worship
© depositphotos/DesignPicsInc

Music, Digital Arts, and Film.[33] Vanguard University, located in California, also offers degrees in the arts.

Hillsong Church. Founded in Australia in 1983, Hillsong Church now has 12 sites around the world.[34] The arts have been incorporated extensively within the church, especially in the development of praise and worship music. Hillsong College offers arts-related certificate, diploma, and advanced diploma in ministry degrees in Worship Music, Dance, Production, and TV and Media.[35]

Presbyterian Church, USA. The role of the arts and worship, for the Presbyterian Church, USA, is tied to the artist's calling in Christ. For this denomination, it involves a calling and new life in Christ, as well as gifts given by the Holy Spirit including among other things, curiosity, imagination, dance, poetry, and drama.[36]

The Presbyterian Association of Musicians is a national organization of the denomination for those working in the areas of worship, music, and the arts. The organization hosts conferences on worship and music, posts jobs, assists with financial grants, publishes *Call to Worship* as well as booklets, awards certification for musicians, and hosts an online forum.[37] Perhaps one of the most well-known among many of the Presbyterian Churches educational institutions offering arts programs is Belhaven University. Belhaven's School of the Arts offers bachelor's degrees in Visual Art, Arts Administration, Creative Writing, Dance, Graphic Design, Music and Theatre.[38] While not a complete list, a sampling of other Presbyterian institutions offering arts courses is Sterling College, Queens University of Charlotte, Macalester College, Stillman College, and Davidson College.

Saddleback Church. Founded some 33 years ago by Rick Warren, Saddleback Church integrates the arts in numerous ways in the life of the congregation including Worship Band, Technical Arts, Vocal Ministry, Worship Arts Ministry, Graphic Arts Ministry, Saddleback Academy of Music, and Urban Arts Outreach.[39] The most recent arts initiative, Ex Creatis Arts is an arts initiative intended for "creating a center for artists to come together and serve, using our individual creative talents to speak as a collective group and spark imagination, connection, and illumination."[40] Projects have included exhibits, and installations; art forms utilized throughout the organization include music, dance, singing, visual arts, technical arts, and production.

Southern Baptist. With a membership of nearly 16 million in America,[41] a number of the Southern Baptist affiliated colleges and seminaries offer degrees in the arts. Baylor University, Belmont University, Cedarville University, Dallas Baptist University, Samford University, and Shorter University, just to name a few.[42] The world's largest Evangelical university, Liberty University's School of Communication and Creative Arts offers degrees in Cinematic Arts, Digital Media and Communication Arts, Theatre Arts, and Studio and Digital Arts.[43] Liberty's School of Music includes degrees in Artist Development, Music and Worship Studies, Piano Performance, Songwriting and String Performance, among others.[44] Located in Louisville, Kentucky, Southern Baptist Theological Seminary's Doctor of Philosophy degree provides research opportunities in Christianity and the Arts.

Willow Creek Community Church. Located near South Barrington, Illinois, Willow Creek Community Church has helped set the standard in arts integration in the local congregation. As part of its core values, the church encourages cultural engagement through the arts, using 1 Corinthians 9:19-23 as a scriptural basis.[45]

Willow Creek offers service opportunities for the following teams—Music, Dance, Media, Production, Communication Photography, and Visual Arts.[46] Many other churches, including NorthRidge Church, Plymouth, Michigan; Northland, A Church Distributed, Longwood, Florida; and LifeChurch, Edmond, Oklahoma; representing many denominations and affiliations could be discussed.

While not an exhaustive list, the forgoing examples illustrate the increased integration of the arts on the local, national and international level. At the same time, regional and national para-church organizations have developed for purposes of community enrichment, outreach, education, and ultimately to bring glory to God through the arts.

NINE

Global Arts Networks and Renewal

"However, in recent years a growing number of these same communities have begun to manifest a new interest in the arts and have made significant moves forward in engaging the arts in the life of the church. To be sure, it has not been a total transformation, but the signs are clear that a renaissance in the arts is taking place among churches in the west."
—LAUSANNE MOVEMENT OCCASIONAL PAPERS

Reverend Billy Graham
Courtesy of Library of Congress

The Arts: A Global Renewal

This book concludes with a look at the worldwide expansion of the arts in Christianity. Within a little over a decade of the new century and new millennium, the role of the arts in Christianity has changed significantly. When contrasted with the integration of the arts at the dawn of the twentieth century, the difference is phenomenal. Many reasons could be given for this, but from all indications this is a sovereign move of the Lord to renew the arts within the church.

The growing influence of the Evangelical Movement, coupled with the Liturgical Renewal Movement, Jesus Movement, and Charismatic Movement, dramatically changed the religious landscape of Christianity around the world after mid-century. As mentioned previously, the evangelistic crusades of Billy

Graham and Oral Roberts, among others, had far-reaching influence, especially with the use of television and radio. Other ministries, with similar purposes, developed as well. As early as 1969, Cam Floria took The Continentals abroad, initially starting with concerts in Europe. This group, which had humble beginnings in California, would eventually have an international impact on the renewal of Christian involvement with the arts. Floria, who was a composer, musician, and choir director, had worked with Youth for Christ in 1963 when he created the touring group The Continental Singers. In the same year, he released the pop music tinged chorus album "Sing A Happy Song", which met with immediate success. Numerous albums were released in the wake of the initial release and featured the latest songs and music of the time.[1]

The Continentals first outreach was to the Netherlands, in cooperation with author and theologian Leen LaRiviere. This tour was a huge success and would be the foundation for monumental changes in Christian interaction with the arts in Europe and beyond. By 1974, Floria created the Christian Artists Seminar in Colorado. Also in 1974, LaRiviere created the first non-American Continentals group. This was followed by the creation of German, French, Italian, Hungarian, Slovak, and Romanian Continental groups. In all, 25 European Continental groups were created, as well as 400 concerts reaching 100,000 people per year, a leadership training school, and 500 students in training. Divisions include Continental Kids, Young Continentals, Continental Orchestra, and Continental Encores.[2] Worldwide 60 groups are on the road each year. Since its beginning more than 15 million people have been reached. Following the pattern set by Floria's Christian Artists Seminar in America, LaRiviere created the Christian Artists Seminar in Europe in the early 1980s, of which The Continentals became a part. By the mid-1980s, dance, mime, and theater were added, with visual arts included by the late 80s.[3] As major cultural changes took place during the 80s in Europe, the organization refocused its vision for the future. The resulting sociocultural emphasis for the arts is summarized in the following statement:

The evangelistic crusades of Billy Graham and Oral Roberts, among others, had far-reaching influence, especially with the use of television and radio.

Europe is our target; because Europe will change in the nineties. Those changes will help to create a new openness. This openness is important for a new time, where values have meaning again. So we believe in a future revival, a new breakthrough of the Holy Spirit, a "later rain" pouring on each section of society. The Lord has led us to look at all the factors that could slow down or speed up this process.

In 1990, LaRiviere founded The International Association of Christian Artists (IACA), which by 1992 was comprised of over 100 organizations and 4,000 affiliated members.[4] The IACA now has member organizations in 34 nations around the world. Countries include Australia, Belgium, Brazil, Bulgaria, Canada, Czechia, Denmark, Finland, France, Germany, Greece, Hungary, Indonesia, Ireland, Italy, Japan, Latvia, Lithuania, Malta, Nepal, Netherlands, Philippines, Poland, Portugal, Puerto Rico, Romania, Slovakia, South Africa, South Korea, Spain, Sweden, Switzerland, United Kingdom, and the United States.[5]

In 1970, about the same time that Floria developed The Continentals, Byron Spradlin began planning for an arts ministry that he hoped would have far reaching influence. In his own words, his assignment was "to disciple and mentor people out of music and the arts, working them into the fabric of Church, Missions & Marketplace ministry around the world."[6] 1972 found Spradlin volunteering with Campus Crusade for Christ leading worship, as well as participating in summer music evangelism teams in 20 nations with The Continentals.

In 1973 Spradlin founded Hineni Ministries and by 1976 became Artists in Christian Testimony International, making this ministry one of the first of its type in America. By 1980, ACT International was focused specifically on missions and the arts. In 1990, it became one of the first interdenominational missionary organizations to send out arts ministry and missionary specialists. The group has specialists in areas such as Craft Arts, Dance, Mime, Drama, Theatre, Fashion, Textile, Film, Video, Television, Radio, Literary Arts, Journalism, Music Performance, Production, Songwriting, Speaking, Teaching, Story-Telling, Technical Arts, Sound, Lighting, Visual Arts, Graphic Design, and Photography. Artist in Christian Testimony International currently oversees 188 ministry Departments and 265 people in 20 countries including Asia, Brazil, Canada, Germany, Great Britain, France, Hungary, Israel, Italy, Japan, Kazakhstan, Kenya,

Lebanon, Middle East, North Africa countries [creative access areas], Rwanda, Russia, South Africa, Spain and Uganda, and in 32 States in the USA.[7]

A year later in 1971, London based Arts Centre Group, which was the vision of actor Nigel Goodwin, was formed. Goodwin, who graduated from the Royal Academy of Dramatic Arts and studied under Francis Schaeffer and Hans Rookmaker, is the founder and executive director of the Genesis Arts Trust.[8] The vision of the group is to "support artists in every arts discipline in integrating faith, life and artistic endeavor"[9] The organization has been governed by patrons and directors from a variety of arts professions, including music, dance, television, theater, radio, ministers, writers, and composers.[10]

In 1978, Mary Jones founded the Christian Dance Fellowship in Australia.

In 1978, Mary Jones founded the Christian Dance Fellowship in Australia. By 1987, Jones had visions of an international organization for dancers, which became a reality in 1988 with the creation of the International Christian Dance Fellowship (ICDF). In 1991, 16 countries attended the first ICDF conference in Jerusalem.[11] The ICDF provides opportunities for members across the globe according to network in areas such as ballroom dance, creative arts and social concerns, dance artists, dance for children, dance movement therapy and healing, dance teachers, deaf signing, flags and banners, men in dance, messianic dance and tambourine, missions, movement meditation, and prayer network.[12] ICDF has partnered with Unity College of Australia to offer diplomas in dance.[13]

Countries that are part of the ICDF include Australia, Fiji, Singapore, Malaysia, Korea, Indonesia, Philippines, Japan, Britain, Germany, Ireland, Sweden, France, Italy, Holland, Ghana, South Africa, Kenya, Costa Rica, Jamaica, Puerto Rico, Suriname, St. Maarten, Argentina, Trinidad, Virgin Islands, Canada, and the United States of America.[14]

In Switzerland, a Bible study held in 1985 by students at the Music Academy of Basel led to the creation of an international music organization called Crescendo, which is a part of Campus Crusade for Christ/Agape Europe ministry. Nearly 60 faculty offer courses through Crescendo's annual Summer Institute with numerous courses and workshops for voice and opera, instruments for chamber music and orchestra, piano accompanying, solo studies, jazz, and choral conducting. Crescendo works among classical professional musicians and students, and is active internationally in Asia, Australia, Canada, Germany, Hungary, India, Russia, South Africa, Switzerland, and America.

An organization with a long history of international outreach, Youth with a Mission (YWAM) was founded in 1960 and is now active in 149 countries. Among the organizations many evangelistic strategies over the years have been to utilize the arts in various forms such as street dramas and worship teams. The founding of the University of Nations in 1989 provided a formalized structure for arts training, focusing on dance, drama, and performing arts. Today, associate, bachelor, and master degrees with a staggering number of training opportunities in areas such as music, worship, dance, performing arts, fine arts, film and media, and photography are included in the university curriculum and offered around the globe.[15]

In 1991, the *Art and Christianity* Enquiry Trust was established in London, England, and hosted its first international conference titled "Art-Theology-Church." Since its inception, conferences have been held internationally in Germany, America, France, Russia, and the Netherlands. A quarterly journal "Art and Christianity" began publication in 1995 providing information on exhibitions, events, and book reviews related to art and religion. The organization encourages exhibition of art in churches, as well as documenting important works of art in British churches and cathedrals.[16]

By 1995, Creative Arts Europe, headquartered in Belgium, was established by Jim and Anne Mills. As early as 1985, the Mills' had worked with the performing arts group Project Exalt! and traveled across Europe. In 1990, CAE held its first summer arts session. Another outreach effort, Next Generation Arts and Creativity, was intended to inspire young artists to serve God through the arts. In 1995, the first Art House was established in Belgium, with others developed afterwards in Germany and Switzerland. In 1996, CEA established

Pope John Paul II
© Eddie Adams/Corbis

Xaris Dance Company in Germany, and has conducted workshops as well as performances in schools and festivals in Germany, Austria, and Finland. Creative Arts Europe is now involved in a number of arts outreaches throughout Europe and America including seminars, tours, exhibitions, and cultural programs.[17]

As the new millennium approached, Pope John Paul II spoke directly to artists worldwide extending an appeal to reconsider their vocation. His remarkable 1999 homily, *A Letter Of His Holiness Pope John Paul II To Artists*, was written to "all who are passionately dedicated to the search for new 'epiphanies' of beauty so that through their creative work as artists they may offer these as gifts to the world." The Pope had a long-standing affinity with the arts, having studied drama in his youth and was one of the pioneers of "Rhapsodic Theatre" in Krakow during the 1940s.[18] In one of the most profound segments of the document, he states:

> With this Letter, I turn to you, the artists of the world, to assure you of my esteem and to help consolidate a more constructive partnership between art and the Church. Mine is an invitation to rediscover the depth of the spiritual and religious dimension which has been typical of art in its noblest forms in every age. It is with this in mind that I appeal to you, artists of the written and spoken word, of the theatre and music, of the plastic arts and the most recent technologies in the field of communication. I appeal especially to you, Christian artists: I wish to remind each of you that, beyond functional considerations, the close alliance that has always existed between the Gospel and art means that you are invited to use your creative intuition to enter into the heart of the mystery of the Incarnate God and at the same time into the mystery of man.[19]

In this letter, the Pope touched on numerous topics such as the artist, image of God the Creator, the special vocation of the artist, the artistic vocation in the service of beauty, the artist, and the common good. Remembering Vatican II he stated:

> The Second Vatican Council laid the foundation for a renewed relationship between the Church and culture, with immediate implications for the world of art. This is a relationship offered in friendship, openness and dialogue.[20]

The Pope was careful to appeal to all artists, those who are writers, speakers, actors, musicians, sculptors, and those involved in communication technology, specifically calling on artists to accept the Holy Spirits role in artistic inspiration:

> Every genuine inspiration, however, contains some tremor of that "breath" with which the Creator Spirit suffused the work of creation from the very beginning. Overseeing the mysterious laws governing

the universe, the divine breath of the Creator Spirit reaches out to human genius and stirs its creative power. He touches it with a kind of inner illumination which brings together the sense of the good and the beautiful, and he awakens energies of mind and heart which enable it to conceive an idea and give it form in a work of art.[21]

The growth of the arts among Christians around the world, and the uniquely cultural role these forms of art take, is at the heart of the International Council of Ethnodoxologists (ICE). Founded in 2003 by Paul Neeley and Robin Harris, the vision of ICE is to "encourage and equip Christ followers in every culture to express their faith through their own heart music and other arts."[22] Further, Creatives in cultures around the world are encouraged to interact with the arts by "showing appreciation for the various creative expressions found in local communities; participating in local forms of music-making, dancing, sculpting, acting, painting, storytelling and so forth; studying local forms of artistic expression and their meanings; and catalyzing the creation of culturally relevant and biblically appropriate music and other arts in the life of the local church."[23]

Frank Fortunato, who founded Heart Sounds International, a music and arts ministry of Operation Mobilization, serves as Vice-President of ICE. Fortunato has also taught at the Webber Institute Center for Global Worship Renewal.[24]

In the late 1950s, George Verwer's vision of Operation Mobilization International (OM) became a reality. Within a few years of its founding, the group had 2,000 people involved in summer outreach to Europe, and 6,100 workers around the world today in 118 countries. Recognizing the compelling power of the arts in demonstrating the gospel, OM birthed Operation Mobilization Arts International, (OM Arts) a ministry of OM that was founded in 2009 by Bill Drake with other artist missionaries in OM, in order to "empower artists to engage their creative gifts in exalting God and extending His Kingdom among

Operation Mobilization Arts International was founded in 2008 to "empower artists to engage their creative gifts in exalting God and extending his kingdom among the nations."

the nations". As part of it's outreach efforts, OM Arts has created a multifaceted approach to arts ministries: facilitation of short-term mission trips for artists as artists, long-term international field placements for artists in residence, and specialized training for artists who feel called to become missionaries as artists. Artslink, Dancelink, OM Arts Theater, Heart Sound International, Bill Drake Band, and Jon Simpson Music take artists into mission. The OM Arts School of Mission, and Incarnate 2012 and 2014, have helped prepare artists for long-term placement on the mission field in over 11 countries to date.[25]

The Lausanne Movement, a worldwide network of evangelical leaders focused on missions, has recently acknowledged the crucial role the arts play in the life of the church, evangelism, and culture around the world. The impetus for this perspective was actually formed in the "Lausanne Covenant,"

The Lausanne Covenant urged Christians to transform and enrich culture for God's glory.

written in 1974 at the first Lausanne Conference, held in Lausanne Switzerland. The covenant addressed a number of topics, but of particular interest here is the statement on evangelism and culture, which recognized "beauty and goodness" as a product of common grace found in cultures around the world. It also urged Christians to transform and enrich culture for God's glory.[27]

By 2004, a significant document regarding the arts, culture, and the church was produced by one of the conference's issue groups. Titled "Redeeming the Arts: The Restoration of the Arts to God's Creational Intention," this could be considered one of the landmark documents of the last 100 years regarding the relationship of the church, especially evangelical churches, to the arts. As the prologue states:

> For an established and respected mission organization to recognize the arts as strategic to the life and mission of the church, and to commission a paper about the arts in the context of faith and redemption, is both visionary and long overdue. Apart from a small number of important voices, the church as a whole has been virtually silent on the topic for generations.[28]

The document further proposed areas in which the church can nurture the arts, including education and discipleship, as well as spiritual and cultural transformation. One of the most compelling statements of the document addresses the recent renaissance of the arts in the church:

> *However, in recent years a growing number of these same communities have begun to manifest a new interest in the arts and have made significant moves forward in engaging the arts in the life of the church. To be sure, it has not been a total transformation, but the signs are clear that a renaissance in the arts is taking place among churches in the west.*[29]

The convener of the issue group was writer, director, and producer Colin Harbinson, one of the leading voices calling for arts renewal in the church over the last 40 years. The co-convener was Mary Jones, founder of International Christian Dance Fellowship. Nearly 40 additional contributors from 14 countries worked on the document.

Within six years, the issue group's exploratory arts document played a part in formulating the confession produced by the Lausanne group. In 2010, the Lausanne Conference convened in Cape Town, South Africa, in what Christianity Today called "the most representative gathering of Christian leaders in the 2000 year history of the Christian movement."[30] Among the conference attendees were 4,200 evangelical leaders from 198 countries. One of the most significant accomplishments of the gathering was the Cape Town Commitment, which was a confession of faith and action by the delegation covering a wide range of theological and practical topics. Two previous affirmations of this type had been made, the Lausanne Covenant in 1974 and the Manila Manifesto in 1989. Of particular interest here is the confession on "Truth and the Arts in Mission" which, in essence, called the international body of Christ to action in the arts. It reads:

> *We possess the gift of creativity because we bear the image of God. Art in its many forms is an integral part of what we do as humans and can reflect something of the beauty and truth of God. Artists at their best are truth-tellers and so the arts constitute one important way in which we can speak the truth of the gospel. Drama, dance, story, music*

and visual image can be expressions both of the reality of our brokenness, and of the hope that is centered in the gospel that all things will be made new.[31]

The statement also emphasized the mission aspect of the arts and suggested practical strategies such as bringing arts back into the faith community, supporting believing artists, allowing the arts to be an outreach to others, and respecting indigenous culture expressions.[32] After the 2010 Conference, 40 contributors were asked to formulate bibliographic resources for understanding the Commitment. Of those, three had direct input on the arts—John Franklin, Matthew Niermann, and Byron Spradlin.[33]

By 2011, the World Evangelical Alliance, which was founded in 1846 and now represents 600 million Evangelicals worldwide, sponsored *Arts in Mission: Training for Cross-Cultural Ministry*, designed to "effectively engage music and the arts in cross-cultural contexts."[34] Held at All Nations Christian College in the United Kingdom, partnering organizations included the ICE, SIL International, All Nations Christian College, and Mission Commission of WEA. Other participating organizations included Operation Mobilization, Artists in Christian Testimony International, and WEC International. According to the event press release, "over 60 arts advocates and practitioners from 20 nations gathered for the event."[35]

In 2012, the Lausanne Movement appointed Byron Spradlin as a Senior Associate for the Arts, demonstrating, in the words of Executive Director Reverend Douglas S. Birdsall, "the deep commitment Lausanne has to the involvement of artistic Christians in mission and world evangelization."[36] By 2013, The Lausanne Movement Consultation on Arts in Mission was held at the Graduate Institute of Applied Linguistics in Dallas, Texas. Partnering with the Lausanne Movement were The World Evangelical Alliance, and the ICE. Goals are in place to continue seeking opportunities for arts integration in cultures around the world.

From its inception, the church has used art and artists to tell the story of the gospel, and thereby shape culture. Throughout the twentieth century the church has witnessed the impact of Creatives who have heard the call to art as a vocation. Across a wide range of cultures this message has been expressed in multiple art forms. Along the way new concepts were developed which transformed ways of interpreting music, visual art, dance, theatre, technology and story. An artistic language was developed over time that transcends culture. Both the ecclesiastical and secular spheres, triumphs of faith, life and death, heaven and hell, have been depicted through the arts. In many ways these individuals have attempted, through prayer, calling and love for God, to embody an aesthetic that appealed to both the natural and spiritual. Collectively, their art has formed a global movement that is shaping villages, cities, states and nations.

Pioneer Creative Catalyst's Story

Rev. Dr. Byron Spradlin,
President of Artists in Christian Testimony International

The Rev. Dr. Byron Spradlin is founder and president of Artists in Christian Testimony Intl, a missions & ministry sending board for artists and creatives. He has directed this ministry since it's founding in 1973. As of June, 2014, Dr. Spradlin oversees 184 Ministry Departments and 266 people [54 full time staff, 56 part-time staff (bi-vocational), 68 active volunteers, 75 On-going Project Staff, 2 Staff Candidates, and 11 short-term missions volunteers] doing ministry in 23 countries, and in 33 States in America. A.C.T. Intl is also incorporated in Canada and Brazil. Dr. Spradlin also works with mission agencies and churches to help them become more friendly places for artists. Since surrendering his life to Christ's service at 19, God has used Dr. Spradlin, as a musician, recording artist, published songwriter (ASCAP & NARAS), youth pastor, worship pastor, evangelist, church planter, senior pastor, Bible teacher, and professor.

Dr. Spradlin is a graduate of Western Seminary, Portland, Oregon; with a Master of Divinity degree (heavy in Missions, and biblical languages). While there he was the co-founder of the Master of Church Music degree—which he also received there, and for which he served on adjunct faculty for two years in the late 1970's. He and did the class work for the Master of Theology degree at Fuller Theological Seminary. In 2012, he was awarded the Doctor of Ministry degree (in Worship Studies) from Liberty Baptist Theological Seminary, Liberty University, in Lynchburg, Virginia – where he has also taught classes from time to time in the Worship Studies department.

Over the years Dr. Spradlin has become an international specialist on the theology of worship, imagination and arts leadership. He regularly disciples artists; and encourages pastors and missionaries concerning arts and music in ministry and missions.

Dr. Spradlin serves as the international Senior Associate for the Arts for the global Lausanne Committee for World Evangelization. He Chairs the School of Worship, Imagination & the Arts at Williamson College in Franklin Tennessee. Dr. Spradlin is also the Vice-Board-Chair of the international Jews for Jesus mission, having previously served 35 years as Board Chair and the performance coach for their music-evangelism team, The Liberated Wailing Wall. He is also the President of ACT Music Group, Inc. Since 2014, he has been serving on the Board of World Venture mission agency based in Denver, Colorado.

His ministry experience ranges through almost 50 nations, and from arts in evangelism, missions and ministry, to Jewish & Muslim Evangelism, church planting, worship ministry and coaching, and the theology of worship, imagination and the arts. His heart is to see people find forgiveness and rightness with God through Jesus Christ, and grow in a companioning worship walk with HIM daily as they live out a culture-changing life of service for HIM in their community.

Dr. Spradlin has been married for 40 years to his wife Pam; he has two children and four amazing grand children.

Byron@ACTinternational.org
http://www.facebook.com/#!/byron.spradlin
Twitter @byronspradlin

Pioneer Creative Catalyst's Story

Steve Scott,
Director, Christian Artists Networking Association

Crying for a Vision: A Personal Essay

Recently, I have been telling people that much of my ongoing learning about art, culture and matters of faith forms a pattern around a couple of significant events.

In the late 1980s I went to Bali Indonesia, to take part in an arts conference. What I saw then, and during subsequent visits had a profound impact on me. I saw a variety of local cultural expressions in which art and life were tightly integrated. Artistic forms, social values and underlying spiritual concerns were woven together in ways that not only provided a tapestry of a living (and changing) tradition but also the beginnings of a possible vocabulary for those of us wishing to speak about culture, creativity, redemption and restoration.

Here is the other significant event. Four years ago I made a trip to Colmar, France and I spent several days visiting the Unterlinden museum in order to spend time with Grunewald's multi paneled Isenheim Altarpiece. This altarpiece had been commissioned for installation in an Antonite monastery involved in the care of those suffering from a terrible wasting illness. The artist had gone to great pains to portray a Christ who was an empathic co sufferer with those being cared for in this place. The artist also wove many contextually nuanced symbols into the different panels. These would have been 'read' and appreciated by the victims of this illness as they viewed the different panels during the celebration of the Eucharist.

These two experiences, my time in Bali, and my time spent with the Isenheim altarpiece in France have influenced how I now think about my own learning journey when it comes to matters of art and faith.

One more thing before we get going… I also mention lots of names throughout what I am about to tell you. This is less about 'who I know' (hopefully) and more about the importance of personal relationships, partnerships and how much we can learn from and help one another in our shared quest for a faithful approach to arts and culture.

I am British. I grew up in North East London. In 1967 I became a believer via a local Evangelical Free Church mission. This happened as I was leaving high school and enrolling in my foundation year at art school. This was also the time of the UK response to 'the summer of love' elsewhere. I watched the emergence of the alternative hippie subculture, psychedelic rock music, radical politics, and alternative spiritualties….and of course the emerging rumblings of what would be called 'post modernism' in culture and the arts. At the beginning of the 1970s, the (London) Arts Centre Group under the leadership of Nigel Goodwin provided a 'third space' and a framework for an exploration and discussion of both the culture at large and some of the more nuanced, intelligent Christian responses to it.

This 'third space' plus the incisive writing and intelligent theological and cultural analysis of people like Francis Schaeffer and Hans Rookmaaker had some significant impact on the thinking and practice of those of us trying to get our thinking straight on art, culture and faith at that time. It was elements like this, plus my exposure to the nascent 'Jesus movement' that influenced my next choices.

Around 1972/3, while at art school I met a visiting American singer songwriter named Randy Stonehill. I appreciated his work, and he listened to and liked some of the music I was writing then. He introduced my work to a friend of his called Larry Norman, popularly regarded as `the father of Jesus Rock'. Around that time, he was laying the groundwork for a record label he was starting. As the label (Solid Rock) grew in the mid to late 1970s it included such artists as Mark Heard and Tom Howard.

Meanwhile, I finished art school in the mid-1970s, just as the explosive `anti culture' of punk rock sent shock waves through the establishment. …Including the now established and somewhat commodified alternative subculture of the 1960s.

My art school experience and my early years as a believer were marked by those two social/cultural upheavals…the ` 1960s alt/hippie 'one and the aggressive `punk rock' one of the mid-1970s. I had also joined many others in trying to figure out a sane Christian response to the social and cultural changes unfolding around us. When I was done with art school I moved to the USA to begin making a record for Larry Norman's record label.

Once in the USA I became exposed not only to the issues of faith and culture that were being discussed in the context of `Jesus Rock' music, but I continued my own exploration and learning about the larger world of postmodern art. After some months in the Los Angeles area I moved to Northern California to work with a church that was exploring the different ways of approaching and using the arts as an expression of faith. I joined the staff at this church, Warehouse Ministries, an affiliate of Calvary Chapel. Lots of things came out of the innovative explorations at Warehouse Ministries under the creative and pastoral leadership of Mary and Louis Neely. There were weekly music concerts as part of the church's outreach. There were also poets, dramatists, visual artists and dancers all trying on new ways of thinking about the relationship between art and faith. Exit records came out of that time, with artists like Charlie Peacock, the 77s and Vector, among others. I learned, and continue to learn a lot from my time there, both in terms of artistic expression and also other forms of ministry.

I was continuing to explore my own artistic expressions in poetry and mixed media. I was also publishing a number of articles and being invited to teach about arts and faith in a variety of settings. On one occasion in the mid-1980s I had gone to southern California to teach for a week in a summer school on arts and mission. It was during this week that I learned from my hosts, Gene and Mary Lou Totten of the formation of an organization that was intended to connect and network artists and creative workers in places like Africa, the

Philippines and South East Asia (and elsewhere) This 'Traditional Media Unit' of the International Christian Media Commission. Was taking shape under the leadership of Kathleen and Bruce Nicholls.

There was a newsletter, and some international conferences. I went to the first one on the island of Bali in 1989, and have been involved with the organization ever since. It was also at that first conference in Bali that I met Esther Augsburger who took a subsequent significant leadership role with the TMU working with the artists from Eastern Europe. The different threads of my experience of working with a church, creating my own art, and teaching and writing about arts and culture led me to a place where I was asked to take leadership of TMU in 2002. I renamed it CANA (Christian Artists Networking Association.) We have continued the work of connecting and networking artists and we hold conferences in places like Bali, Bulgaria and (upcoming) Cambodia. These experiences became stepping-stones along a path that led to other opening doors.

In the early 1990s I was teaching in the 'Artrageous" arts track at the Cornerstone rock festival in Illinois. Here I met Colin Harbinson, founder and president of International Arts Festivals, who was also teaching on the arts. As a result of the relationship that grew out of that meeting I was able to participate in the international arts events he was organizing in places like St Petersburg, Russia in 1992…. and the People's Republic of China in 1999. I was also able to join the arts concern group that Colin oversaw during the Lausanne World Evangelization conference in Pattaya, Thailand in 2004. John Franklin and Byron Spradlin were part of that group also. Partially as a result of relationships seeded, nurtured and built within that group, the organization CANA is now a ministry department of the organization Artists in Christian Testimony International. (President: Byron Spradlin)

There are more stories I could tell, and people I should acknowledge. Currently I am continuing to explore ideas, build relationships, connect with and learn from others in a rapidly changing and globally networked world. Our ideas about art history, practice and cultural legacy will (or should) continue to change in a world where the centers of economic power are dramatically shifting. Other economies and other cultures are in their ascendant phase. (Eurocentric) Postmodernism has given way to (Global)'multiple modernity's' according to one source.

We should also recognize that the church, according to some, is now weighted towards 'the majority world'. There are more Christians there than here. What can we learn from artists of faith working in and with very different cultural contexts and traditions?

I believe that we are standing on the edge of a number of vital opportunities for growing in our faithful learning, understanding and practice of cultural engagement. My art school experience in the 1960s/70s introduced me to postmodernism' and `multiculturalism'. Many years of working in and with the local church helped me to understand some of the issues people grapple with as they try and relate their faith to art. The creative work and critical writing and teaching that I have attempted have been shaped by that learning as well as what I have seen in South East Asia and elsewhere.

But as I said at the beginning, it is really my time in Bali, and my time with the Isenheim altarpiece in Colmar, France that currently guides my conversation about the arts in the context of our faith. These two events are like lenses through which I try to look at everything else. They are also like lights guiding my steps along a path that is providentially nuanced and richly informed by a number of personal connections and relationships. To learn more go here: **https://cryingforavision.wordpress.com/**

Pioneer Creative Catalyst's Story

John Franklin,
Executive Director, Imago
Toronto, Canada

Art and the Divine Call Creative Imagining

The last three decades has witnessed significant changes within the evangelical community among which is a new openness to the arts. A quick survey of the history or visual art and music in the Western culture will provide ample evidence of the intimate connection between art and Christian faith. Protestantism has been known for its scepticism about the arts, particularly the visual arts. It has been characteristic of Protestantism that it gives attention to "word" rather than image. And so we find the focus on preaching and note that our churches are generally image free – except perhaps for a simple cross. Both the Orthodox and the Catholic tradition have been more open to the presence of images believing they are valuable for the practice of worship and spiritual instruction. Current trends within protestant evangelicalism evidence a return to this long established tradition of drawing on images for worship and as a means to enrich the spiritual journey.

The first part of my career was spent teaching philosophy at a Christian college in Toronto Canada. Since 1998 I have served as Executive Director of Imago – an organization which seeks to be an advocate for arts and for Christian artists in Canada. Imago was founded in 1972 and was thus well ahead of the wave of interest in the arts we see today. Imago embraces an Evangelical theology and has a mandate to exercise a biblically-based influence on Canadian culture. My work with artists has led me into extended study and reflection on themes related to theology and the arts.

I have come in contact with many who hold to a negative view of the arts harbouring suspicion and fear of the arts. We still hear the voice that alerts us to the potential dangers of the theatre, music, images and even of human imagination. It is true that these things can be a source of temptation and diversion from the narrow way we are called to walk. Yet what is surprising is that scripture itself takes up artistic expression in parable, poetry, narrative, and image and invites the imagination to engage its truths and its stories. It's worth noting that those first said to be filled with "divine spirit" were artists. (Exodus 35:30 – 36:1)

In the early chapters of Genesis we read of the invitation—to be fruitful, multiply, care for and steward the earth. This has been called the cultural mandate. The spirituality we are to embrace is not just a matter of inward experience but has an outward dimension as well. To be redeemed means that we are in covenant relationship with God and in that light we are to recognize our responsibilities to both nature and culture.

Just as God has called the world into order (Genesis 1 and 2) humanity is mandated to bring an order to the world that is God-honouring. The call to order the world is an affirmation of the goodness of creation. Art is one means through which we express our understanding of how the world is ordered and how it ought to be.

In 2004 I was invited to participate in a consultation hosted by Lausanne International. It was a gathering of about 1500 that took place in Thailand. There were about thirty five groups with twenty to fifty participants in each all on different topics related to global mission. Our group of about forty was gathered under the theme *Redeeming the Arts*. The discussion and the subsequent document focused on three topics believed to be essential for furthering the conversation on arts and mission: Art and a Renewed Theological Vision, Art and Discipleship in the Church, and Art and the

Transformation of Culture. Under the leadership of Colin Harbinson and catalyzed by the forty members of the group, the document was shaped and written by myself along with two fellow Canadians, James Tughan and Phyllis Novak. The final document can be found on the Lausanne International website; www.lausanne.org and is #46 of the Lausanne Occasional Papers (LOPs).

In that document we observed how Evangelicalism has been inclined to measure the value of its activity in terms of its contribution to evangelism. The doctrine of redemption has overshadowed the doctrine of creation and left the arts as valuable only as instruments for spreading the gospel. A more holistic theological understanding looks to creation as well as to incarnation. In so doing it will see the value of creative imagination as a God-given gift to be employed in all of life not least in art-making. There is still much work that needs to be done to deepen our understanding of the place of the arts. Theological themes such as creation and incarnation provide fertile ground for reflection on the arts.

Cultural Context

My work with Imago is done primarily with a face to the culture – seeking to be a cultural presence characterized by vibrant faith and artistic excellence. Although the connection was strong in the past in the nineteenth and early twentieth century artistic expression moved further from religious sensibilities in favour of the rugged individualism of the artist. Dutch art historian Hans Rookmaaker who was influential among evangelicals in the 1960s and 70s, believed in the Lordship of Christ over every area of life— and was instrumental in disciplining a new generation of believers to understand the place of the arts within a biblical worldview. Rookmaaker's strong claim that "art needs no justification" was a reassuring word for many in the evangelical community but left some unconvinced. The majority within evangelicalism continued to neglect the arts, and lacked understanding primarily because of the absence of instruction concerning the place of the arts in the life of faith.

When post modernism showed up it posed a significant challenge to the focus on reason as the final court of appeal for our knowledge. It is now widely accepted that reason – though still important for our understanding of the world – is not the only instrument for our exploration of what is true. Abstract reason must now compete with a focus on "concrete" embodiment and attention to the affections as found in the aesthetic side of life. Postmodernism readily embraces the arts, whether visual art, music, film, poetry, dance or theatre. Or put another way, symbol, narrative and the poetic have become commonly accepted ways to communicate. The new trend brings some balance one sided emphasis inherited from the eighteenth century Enlightenment and often embraced by the church. Examples of the power of art to move both heart and mind is evident both in the world of fine art and popular culture. We are in a transitional moment in history and these important changes must be considered as the faith community seeks to carry out its calling to disciple the nations.

The Arts in Church and Culture

In recent years we have been witness to a growing momentum among evangelicals globally in seeking to weave the arts into the life of the church. In the past thirty years there has been significant growth in Christian arts organizations, conferences, regular gatherings and events all of which are one way or another, focused on the intersection of art and faith. We have also seen the appearance of art galleries, theatre companies, film production, dance troupes, writers' collectives, music groups and innumerable articles and books on art and faith in the evangelical wing of the church. All if this is evidence that evangelicalism is experiencing a renaissance in artistic expression. There are two directions in which these activities flow. One is church-centred the other culture-centred.

Arts and the Church

North American society is deeply influenced by the sounds and images of popular culture. Given the values expressed many Christians have felt uncomfortable embracing those trends. One response has been to develop a sub-culture that offers an alternative to what is found in the mainstream. The idea that Christians should make "Christian art" may be a result of evangelical discomfort with art generally or with art found in the various locations of our culture. The outcome is that art is found acceptable if it has religious content or is employed in the service of evangelism or worship. As an antidote to this inclination we would do well to embrace a more robust doctrine of creation that would result in eliminating the need for legitimizing art through religious practice.

The celebration of the arts taking place in evangelical churches around the globe makes clear that we are on the threshold of a new day. Churches manifest a new openness to art and churches are hiring pastors who are responsible for – arts and worship. In the west the road to bringing arts into the church has had its obstacles. The legacy of the Reformation has engendered some suspicion of the arts and has meant that our worship spaces are simple and unadorned. This is in much contrast to what one may find in the majority world where art is more readily woven into the fabric of ordinary life. Suspicion is still present among western believers, but the involvement in the arts of a younger generation is eroding the suspicion and allowing the arts to be a resource of hope for faith our communities. The arts are being accepted as a context in which one can meet God and experience the divine presence as well as to disclose to us something of God's truth.

Arts and Culture

There is within Evangelical theology an underlying theme that instructs us to "come out from among them". For many this has meant a clear separation from the culture around us. One result of this is that we have failed to learn how to communicate with the culture within which we live. Moreover we have been left with an uncertainty about how best to be "salt and light". Art is one of the places in which we in the church can answer the invitation to be salt and light in a broken and darkened world. Though our art we can speak to the brokenness, the suffering and the darkness – and offer some threads of hope.

My personal reflection on art has led me to the conclusion that all art is inherently hopeful. No matter what its content or who makes it. It is hopeful because it is a product of human imagination and it is God-given imagination that allows us to entertain what is possible, what might be and in that ability is lodges our capacity to hope.

Scripture calls us to faithfulness and faithfulness in not a matter to be measured by "success" or our capacity to change the world. Art is one of the ways we exercise a faithful presence in our particular sphere of life. Trusting that what we do will bear fruit for the sake of the kingdom and for the glory of God. This includes our art-making.

It has recently become more acceptable to see the work of art-making as a legitimate Christian calling. Artists would benefit greatly by receiving the blessing of their communities and in being affirmed in engaging their artistic gift and exercising it with integrity and authenticity. In this way artists might be a kingdom presence in the marketplaces of the world. I would encourage less attention to advocating for art that preaches and more for art that is aesthetically good and tells the truth and I believe that such an approach will serve to strengthen evangelical credibility in the arts.

The image based character of our culture has taken much of its shape from the long-standing influence of film. Space does not permit anything but a mention of this important and influential component of popular culture. There have been a host of books written by evangelicals that discuss film and its significance as a location for exploring moral and spiritual values. Many evangelical publications now carry film reviews which was unheard of two decades ago. The polarization common in the past has now been replaced with a more dialogical approach engaging those with whom we disagree. Art is one bridge for such dialogue. Films, as well as novels, poetry, visual art, theatre and music have become locations for discussion and exploration of things we hold in common as human beings and settings to open conversations on important themes of religious faith.

Arts in Mission

The world of evangelical missions has not in recent times shown much interest in the arts. Art gets little attention from mission leaders though many on the front lines engage the arts in their missional work.

In 2008 the World Evangelical Alliance held meetings in Pattaya Thailand which was followed by a special meeting of the Mission Commission of WEA. At the latter gathering, urged on by the innovative leadership of Bill Taylor and Bertil Ekstrom a Task Force on Arts in Mission was struck. I was privileged to attend those meetings and since 2008 have served as the co-ordinator of that Task Force. A few important projects have come out of the work of the Task Force. One is the publishing a double issue of Mission Commission magazine *Connections* on the theme of Arts in Mission which came out in the fall of 2010 in time for the Lausanne Congress in Cape Town. All the articles give insight into ways in which the arts are being engaged around the globe to carry out the missional task. The fall of 2011 saw a conference held at All Nations Christian College in Hertfordshire England for training in cross cultural mission and exploration of issues related to art and mission. A roundtable on Arts in Mission was held in Dallas Texas in 2013 and the Mission Commission invited an arts focus as part of their global gathering in Izmir Turkey in May 2014.

These more recent developments are but a small piece of the story. Youth with a Mission (YWAM) has for over fifty years exercised a global reach employing innovative strategies for communicating the gospel that has given a major role to the arts. Operation Mobilization has developed a project- OM Arts International seeks to tap the extraordinary resources found in creative artistic imagining and harnesses them for the missional task.

An important expression of arts and mission is found in community arts where those marginalized by mainstream culture or those whose lives have taken a bad turn can find healing and hope. There are scores of projects around the globe set in inner-city contexts which draw the poor, and disenfranchised into a safe context where they can give expression to the pain and hurt in their lives through art making. It may be drama, or dance, visual art or music, poetry or photography, all of which serve to lift some of the burden they bear and contribute to the healing process.

The work I am involved with in Canada under Imago– is designed as a support for artists who are seeking to express their faithfulness by participation in cultural contexts. A jazz pianist has performed with a major symphony orchestra and at numerous jazz festivals across the country. A singer/songwriter and composer undertook a fifteen city tour and received major coverage on national radio and in a national magazine. Another has launched an innovative opera company that is gaining widespread attention and rave reviews. This is but a small piece of what is happening and of what is possible. It is vitally important for Christians to be open to taking their talents and exercising them well beyond the walls of the church so they can be that salt and light presence that has the power to make a difference.

I have been impressed by the number of events in recent times that are shaped in order to give expression to art that is clearly linked to religious belief. During Holy Week in the Spring of 2015 I was privileged to attend a festival of music, visual art and poetry at Kings College Chapel in Cambridge England. It was a week of events that brought the themes of the Passion to fresh attention. And in its own way was a push against the common cultural practice to set religion to the margins. As much as this has been tried it is consistently unsuccessful because religious sensibilities are at the heart of what it is to be human and they cannot be ignored. Those deeply human sensibilities commonly show up in the context of the arts. Art is capable of reaching into the depths of what it means to be human and to open to us new vistas in discovering who we are and what our life means.

What's Ahead?

All of this provides only a glimpse into the wide-ranging activity in the arts among evangelicals. The signs are positive, change is underway, but there is still much to be done. Mention has not been made of the scores of sites on the internet which host conversations and promote artists of faith. One important site is www.artway.eu where you can discover activities and networks around the world. Education is another area which will influence the future for the arts among evangelicals. The Institute for Theology Imagination and the Arts at the University of St. Andrew's in Scotland provides a rich set of programs for those interested in graduate study in theology and the arts and hosts a web presence called Transpositions. There is an active centre at Duke University in Durham North Carolina under the direction of Jeremy Begbie is another sign of promise for the future. There is also the good work of the Brehm Centre at Fuller Theological Seminary.

In conclusion I want to note that art has often become for many a substitute for religion. Museums, theatres, concert halls and stadiums have become sanctuaries for those seeking "spiritual" experiences in a culture where God has been marginalized and is commonly ignored. The answer to this reality is not to run from the arts nor ignore them but rather to set the arts in the broader context of God's good creation and receive them as blessing and gift. Art can be idol or icon. It may become a substitute for God (like so many other things) or a window through which we come to discern more deeply who God is and what God has called us to. It can also be a way to speak the language of hope in a world that lives with uncertainty. There are good signs that evangelicalism is recovering a lost heritage and is becoming attuned to the Spirit's movement through the arts. It has been the focus of my work over the past sixteen years to facilitate, encourage and advocate for artists of faith recognizing the need for salt and light in a world that has lost its moral and spiritual compass. The hope is that a new generation of Christians will take up the challenge and lead the way to renewed engagement and appreciation for the God-given gift of the arts.

John Franklin is Executive Director of Imago (www.imago-arts.on.ca) a Toronto based initiative designed to support Christians in the arts in Canada. He is Chair of the Task Force on Arts and Mission for the WEA - Mission Commission, has been a member (with an arts focus) of the Program Team for Lausanne's Cape Town 2010 and serves as Chair of Lausanne Canada.

ENDNOTES

Chapter One

[1] John H. Vincent, *The Chautauqua Movement* (Boston: Chautauqua Press, 1886), https://archive.org/stream/chautauquamovem00millgoog#page/n302/mode/2up, accessed August 17, 2013.

[2] Ibid, https://archive.org/stream/chautauquamovem00millgoog#page/n180/mode/2up, accessed August 17, 2013.

[3] Ibid.

[4] https://archive.org/stream/chautauquamovem00millgoog#page/n40/mode/2up, accessed August 17, 2013.

[5] http://www.cyberhymnal.org/bio/s/h/e/sherwin_wf.htm, accessed August 17, 2013.

[6] James R. Goff Jr., *Close Harmony: A History of Southern Gospel* (Chapel Hill: University of North Carolina Press, 2002), 37, 51.

[7] Ibid., 37.

[8] http://www.cyberhymnal.org/bio/s/a/n/sankey_id.htm, accessed August 18, 2013.

[9] http://www.christianitytoday.com/ch/131christians/poets/crosby.html?start=2, accessed June 2, 2014.

[10] Abraham Kuyper, Calvinism: Six Stone Lecutures, in the Princeton Theological Seminary Library, https://archive.org/details/calvinismsixst00kuyp, accessed August 20, 2013.

[11] See Susan J. White, *Art, Architecture, and Liturgical Reform: The Liturgical Arts Society 1928–1972* (New York: Pueblo Publishing Company, 1990).

Chapter Two

[1] "The Proceedings of the First Religious Education Association," Chicago, Religious Education Association, 1903, http://archive.org/stream/religiouseducati00reli#page/n5/mode/2up, 351–352, accessed August 17, 2013.

[2] Elias Benjamin Sanford, ed. *Church federation, Inter-church conference on federation* (New York: Fleming H. Revell Company, 1906), http://books.google.com/books?id=UShOAAAAYAAJ&printsec=frontcover&source=gbs_ge_summary_r&cad=0#v=onepage&q&f=false, accessed February 11, 2014.

[3] http://www.wesleyan.edu/library/friends/lib_greats.html, accessed August 18, 2013.

[4] http://www.archive.org/stream/arteducationinpu00haneiala#page/270/mode/2up, accessed August 20, 2013.

[5] http://openlibrary.org/works/OL7793914W/Where_to_go_and_what_to_see, accessed August 19, 2013.

[6] http://www.ifpda.org/content/node/172, accessed August 18, 2013.

[7] http://art.unt.edu/ntieva/HistoryofArtEd/1901-events.html, accessed August 18, 2013.

[8] http://www.livingplaces.com/NY/Chautauqua_County/Chautauqua_Town/Chautauqua_Institution_Historic_District.html, accessed August 21, 2013.

[9] http://www.archive.org/stream/bibleinpractical00reli#page/484/mode/2up, accessed August 23, 2013.

[10] http://www.archive.org/stream/bibleinpractical00reli#page/484/mode/2up, accessed August 23, 2013.

[11] Ibid., 472.

[12] The glory of Lebanon shall come unto thee, the fir tree, the pine tree, and the box together, to beautify the place of my sanctuary; and I will make the place of my feet glorious.

[13] http://www.archive.org/stream/bibleinpractical00reli#page/508/mode/2up, accessed August 25, 2013.

[14] http://www.archive.org/stream/bibleinpractical00reli#page/482/mode/2up, 479–482, accessed August 25, 2013.

[15] http://www.archive.org/stream/bibleinpractical00reli#page/476/mode/2up, 477–482, accessed August 26, 2013.

[16] http://www.archive.org/stream/ministryofart00cramiala#page/viii/mode/2up, viii, accessed August 26, 2013.

[17] http://www.archive.org/stream/ministryofart00cramiala#page/232/mode/2up, 232, accessed August 27, 2013.

[18] http://www.archive.org/stream/ministryofart00cramiala#page/234/mode/2up, 235, accessed August 27, 2013.

[19] http://www.archive.org/stream/ministryofart00cramiala#page/214/mode/2up/search/drama, 215, accessed August 27, 2013.

[20] http://www.sayers.org.uk/dorothy.html, accessed March 4, 2014.

[21] http://www.christianitytoday.com/ch/131christians/musiciansartistsandwriters/sayers.html?start=1, accessed March 4, 2014.

[22] Susan J. White, *Art, Architecture, and Liturgical Reform: The Liturgical Arts Society* 1928–1972 (New York: Pueblo Publishing Company, 1990), 35.

[23] Ibid., 221.

[24] Ibid., 32.

[25] Ibid., 58

[26] Ibid., 69.

[27] http://library.stkate.edu/archives/bethune-caafa#ref69, accessed March 3, 2014.

[28] http://library.stkate.edu/spcoll/ABCade.html, accessed March 4, 2014.

[29] http://www.catholicvirginian.org/archive/2013/2013vol88iss15/pages/profile.html, accessed February 11, 2014.

[30] http://www.npm.org/main/current.html, accessed February 11, 2014.

[31] http://www.catholicvirginian.org/archive/2013/2013vol88iss15/pages/profile.html, accessed February 11, 2014.

[32] http://www.liturgicalconference.org/Liturgical_Conference/Welcome.html, accessed February 11, 2014.

[33] http://www.nationalcouncilofchurches.us/about/, accessed February 11, 2014.

[34] http://history.pcusa.org/collections/findingaids/fa.cfm?record_id=NCC6, accessed March 5, 2014.

[35] http://www.sarcc.org/fellows.htm, accessed March 5, 2014.

[36] http://history.pcusa.org/collections/findingaids/fa.cfm?record_id=NCC6, accessed March 5, 2014.

[37] http://www.dictionaryofarthistorians.org/rookmaakerh.htm, accessed March 4, 2014.

[38] http://www.labri.org/history.html, accessed March 6, 2014.

[39] Francis Schaeffer, Art and the Bible (Downers Grove: Intervarsity Press), 17.

[40] Ibid., 18.

[41] http://www.newnetherlandinstitute.org/history-and-heritage/dutch_americans/nicholas-wolterstorff/, accessed March 10, 2014.

[42] http://www.allofliferedeemed.co.uk/seerveld.htm, accessed March 13, 2014

[43] http://www.talbot.edu/ce20/educators/protestant/frank_gaebelein/, accessed March 14, 2014.

[44] http://www.alliancenet.org/CC/article/0,,PTID307086_CHID564292_CIID1414980,00.html, accessed March 14, 2014.

[45] http://www.colinharbinson.com/bio/index.html, accessed March 15, 2014.

[46] http://www.heartoftheartist.org/about-rory/, accessed March 15, 2014.

[47] http://www.internationalartsmovement.org, accessed March 13, 2014.

[48] http://fujimurainstitute.org

[49] http://www.makotofujimura.com/bio/, accessed June 4, 2014.

[50] http://divinity.duke.edu/initiatives-centers/dita/director, accessed March 16, 2014.

Chapter Three

[1] Laurie F. Maffly-Kipp, Leigh E. Schmidt, and Mark Valeri, *Practicing Protestants: Histories of Christian Life in America*, 1630-1965 (Baltimore: John Hopkins University Press, 2006).

[2] http://www.archive.org/stream/MN41748ucmf_3#page/n31/mode/2up, accessed September 3, 2013.

[3] Martha Candler, *Drama in Religious Service* (New York: New Century Co., 1922), http://www.archive.org/stream/cu31924026102875#page/n13/mode/2up, ix, accessed September 2, 2013.

[4] Ibid., xiii, accessed September 2, 2013.

[5] http://www.archive.org/stream/MN41748ucmf_3#page/n27/mode/2up, 22, accessed September 1, 2013.

[6] http://www.archive.org/stream/MN41748ucmf_3#page/n221/mode/2up, 203, accessed September 4, 2013.

[7] http://www.actorsguild.org/aboutus2.html, accessed September 24, 2013.

[8] Charles S. MacFarland, *The Churches of the Federal Council*, (New York: Fleming H. Revell Company, 1916). http://www.archive.org/stream/churchesoffedera00macf#page/n7/mode/2up, 13, accessed September 5, 2013.

[9] Martha Candler, *Drama in Religious Service* (New York: New Century Co., 1922), http://www.archive.org/stream/cu31924026102875#page/n325/mode/2up. For a full listing see 239–259.

[10] For further information see Candler, 239–259, http://www.archive.org/stream/cu31924026102875#page/n305/mode/2up, accessed September 11, 2013.

[11] Ibid., 114, accessed September 14, 2013.

[12] Maffly-Kipp, Schmidt, and Mark Valeri, *Practicsing Protestants: Histories of Christian Life in America*, 1630-1965 (Baltimore: The Johns Hopkins University Press), 265.

[13] James J. Kempster, ed. *Union Now* (New York: Union Theological Seminary, 2010), 30, accessed September 21, 2013, http://www.utsnyc.edu/document.doc?id=548

[14] Preston Roberts, "The Field of Religion and Art at Chicago," The Christian Scholar 40, no. 41(957): 339–345, accessed September 22, 2013, http://www.jstor.org/discover/10.2307/41177043?uid=3739936&uid=2134&uid=2&uid=70&uid=4&uid=3739256&sid=21102648293191

[15] http://fummwa.affiniscape.com/displaycommon.cfm?an=1&subarticlenbr=13, accessed September 23, 2013.

[16] Larry Eskridge, *Gods Forever Family* (Oxford: Oxford University Press), 92.

[17] http://covenantplayers.org/mission-and-doctrine, accessed September 28, 2013.

[18] http://covenantplayers.org/worldvision, accessed September 28, 2013.

[19] http://adplayers.org/leadership.html, accessed September 28, 2013.

[20] http://adplayers.org/history.html, accessed September 28, 2013.

[21] http://www.lambsplayers.org/about.php, accessed September 28, 2013.

[22] http://www.sight-sound.com/WebSite/history.do, accessed September 28, 2013.

[23] http://www.sight-sound.com/WebSite/mission.do, accessed September 28, 2013.

[24] http://www.sight-sound.com/WebSite/history.do, accessed September 28, 2013.

[25] http://www.acaciatheatre.com/about.php, accessed September 28, 2013.

[26] Ibid., accessed September 28, 2013.

[27] Ibid., accessed September 28, 2013.

[28] http://www.cytsandiego.org/about/, accessed September 28, 2013.

[29] J. Mark Taylor, email correspondence, June 4, 2014.

[30] http://cita.org/site/, accessed October 20, 2013.

[31] http://www.thenightofmiracles.com, accessed July 24, 2014.

[32] http://www.liberty.edu/news/?PID=18495&MID=24579, accessed July 24, 2014.

[33] Numerous denominational websites were searched to obtain this data.

Chapter Four

[1] James R. Goff Jr., *Close Harmony: A History of Southern Gospel* (Chapel Hill: University of North Carolina Press, 2002), 36.

[2] Ibid., 37.

[3] Ibid., 51.df

[4] Ibid., 51.

[5] Ibid., 70.

[6] Ibid., 51.

[7] Ibid., 75.

[8] Ibid., 88.

[9] Ibid., 91.

[10] Ibid.

[11] Ibid., 92.

[12] James R. Goff Jr., *Close Harmony: A History of Southern Gospel* (Chapel Hill: University of North Carolina Press, 2002), 301.

[13] http://gaither.com/artists/bill-gaither, accessed April 12, 2014.

[14] James R. Goff Jr., *Close Harmony: A History of Southern Gospel* (Chapel Hill: University of North Carolina Press, 2002), 28.

[15] http://www.gmahalloffame.org/speaker-lineup/charles-a-tindley/, accessed April 12, 2014.

[16] James R. Goff Jr., *Close Harmony: A History of Southern Gospel* (Chapel Hill: University of North Carolina Press, 2002), 301.

[17] http://www.nashvillesongwritersfoundation.com/d--g/thomas--a--dorsey.aspx, accessed April 12, 2014.

[18] http://www.ncgccinc.com/new/index.php/history/beginnings, accessed April 12, 2014.

[19] http://www.ncgccinc.com/new/index.php/history/dr-thomas-a-dorsey, accessed April 12, 2014.

[20] http://www.georgiaencyclopedia.org/articles/arts-culture/georgia-tom-dorsey-1899-1993, accessed April 12, 2014.

[21] http://www.nashvillesongwritersfoundation.com/d--g/thomas--a--dorsey.aspx, accessed April 12, 2014.

[22] http://gmwanational.net/RevCleveland.htm, accessed April 15, 2014.

[23] http://gmwanational.net/History.htm, accessed April 15, 2014.

[24] https://rockhall.com/inductees/mahalia--jackson/timeline/, accessed April 15, 2014.

[25] W.K. McNeil, Encyclopedia of American Gospel Music (New York: Routledge, Taylor & Francis Group, 2005), accessed January 26, 2014, http://books.google.com/books?id=uqT--CJYcqskC&printsec=frontcover&source=gbs_ge_summary_r&cad=0#v=onepage&q&f=false.

[26] http://www.kirkfranklin.com/biography, accessed January 26, 2014.

[27] http://www.ralphcarmichael.com/bigband.php, accessed January 26, 2014.

[28] http://www.ralphcarmichael.com/biography.php, accessed January 26, 2014.

[29] Barry Alfonso, *The Billboard Guide to Contemporary Christian Music*, (New York: Billboard Books, 2002), 267.

[30] David W. Stowe, *No Sympathy for the Devil* (North Carolina: University of Chapel Hill Press, 2011), 91.

[31] http://www.ccel.us/CCM.ch2.html, accessed February 6, 2014.

[32] http://mindgarage.com/emass1.html, accessed February 2, 2014.

[33] http://www.mindgarage.com/voice.html, accessed February 2, 2014.

[34] Barry Alfonso, *The Billboard Guide to Contemporary Christian Music*, (New York: Billboard Books, 2002), 110.

[35] Barry Alfonso, *The Billboard Guide to Contemporary Christian Music*, (New York: Billboard Books, 2002), 112.

[36] http://www.larrynorman.com, accessed January 26, 2014.

[37] http://www.ccel.us/CCM.ch3.html, accessed January 26, 2014.

[38] http://www.nifty-music.com/stonehill/ccm0890.html, accessed January 28, 2014.

[39] Barry Alfonso, *The Billboard Guide to Contemporary Christian Music*, (New York: Billboard Books, 2002), 193.

[40] Barry Alfonso, *The Billboard Guide to Contemporary Christian Music*, (New York: Billboard Books, 2002), 170.

[41] http://www.michaelwsmith.com/bio.html, accessed February 9, 2014.

[42] Ibid., 138.

[43] http://stevencurtischapman.com/about/, accessed February 9, 2014.

[44] http://www.ccel.us/CCM.ch12.html, accessed January 25, 2014

[45] http://www.centralkynews.com/jessaminejournal/news/ichthus-music-festival-to-return-in-at-kentucky-horse-park/article_7da52098-9f28-5266-a85e-af62aaa70dd8.html, accessed January 21, 2014.

[46] http://www.ccel.us/CCM.ch12.html, Baker, accessed January 26, 2014.

[47] http://creationfest.com/nw/about-us/story/, accessed January 26, 2014.

[48] http://christianartistsseminars.com/staff/, accessed January 26, 2014.

[49] http://www.premierfestivals.com/about, accessed January 26, 2014.

[50] http://bobthompson121.wix.com/cfa-sponsorship#!about-us/csgz, accessed January 26, 2014.

[51] http://www.christianitytoday.com/ch/thepastinthepresent/storybehind/praiseworshiprevolution.html?start=2, accessed April 19, 2014.

[52] http://www.maranathamusic.com/about/, accessed April 19, 2014.

[53] http://www.vineyardworship.com/about, accessed April 19, 2014.

[54] http://www.268generation.com/#!declaration, accessed April 19, 2014.

[55] http://www.darlenezschech.com/biography/, accessed April 19, 2014.

[56] http://www.masterworksfestival.org/vision.html, accessed April 20, 2014.

[57] http://www.masterworksfestival.org/Faculty-Bios_fb7fe16.html, accessed April 21, 2014.

[58] http://www.masterworksfestival.org/Masterworks-Festival-Prospective-Students-Overview.html, accessed April 21, 2014.

Chapter Five

[1] Jay M. Price, *Temples for a Modern God* (Oxford: Oxford University Press, 2013), 28.

[2] Ibid., 28.

[3] Ibid., 29,37.

[4] Ibid., 42.

[5] Ibid., 170.

[6] Ibid., See illustrations in Temples for a Modern God beginning 136.

[7] Ibid., 94.

[8] http://www.catholicartists.co.uk, accessed January 3, 2014.

[9] Susan J. White, *Art, Architecture and Liturgical Reform: The Liturgical Arts Society* 1928–1972 (New York: Pueblo Publishing Company, 1990), 233.

[10] http://www.hildrethmeiere.com/Profile.html, accessed January 3, 2014.

[11] http://www.catholicartistssociety.org/2011/04/, accessed January 3, 2014.

[12] Laurie F. Maffly-Kipp, Leigh E. Schmidt, and Mark Valeri, eds., *Practicing Protestants: Histories of Christian Life in America* 1630–1965 (Baltimore: The Johns Hopkins University Press, 1990), 250–293.

[13] Ibid., 253.

[14] Susan J. White, *Art, Architecture and Liturgical Reform: The Liturgical Arts Society* 1928–1972 (New York: Pueblo Publishing Company, 1990), 159.

[15] http://www.sarcc.org/Halverson.htm, accessed May 7, 2014.

[16] http://civa.org/resources/civa-publications/, accessed May 7, 2014.

[17] Ibid.

[18] http://ecva.org/artists/chapters1.html, accessed May 7, 2014.

[19] Smith, H. Augustine, *Worship in the Church School Through Music, Pageantry and Pictures* (Elgin: David C. Cook Publishing, 1928), 7. At the time of its publication, Smith was the Director of Fine Arts in Religion, in the School of Education and Social Service, Boston University.

[20] Ibid., 125–145.

[21] http://www.christiancomicsinternational.org/pioneers1.html#Anchor-FRANK-49575, accessed January 3, 2014.

[22] http://www.christiancomicsinternational.org/pioneers1.html#Anchor-FRANK-49575, accessed January 3, 2014.

[23] http://www.christiancomicsinternational.org/pace_pioneer.html, accessed January 3, 2014.

[24] http://www.christiancomicsinternational.org/hartley_pioneer.html, accessed January 5, 2014.

[25] http://www.christiancomicsinternational.org/pioneers2.html, accessed January 5, 2014.

[26] http://www.christiancomicsinternational.org/notable1.html, accessed January 5, 2014.

[27] http://www.christiancomicsinternational.org/series_sundaypix.html#anchor-actionbible-2011, accessed January 4, 2014.

[28] http://www.comix35.org/aboutus.html, accessed January 4, 2014.

[29] http://www.christiancomicsinternational.org/series_sundaypix.html#anchor-actionbible-2011, accessed January 4, 2014.

[30] http://www.readthespirit.com/explore/zondervan-publishes-comic-book-revelation/, accessed January 4, 2014.

[31] http://www.kingstonemedia.com/biblecomics.php, accessed January 4, 2014.

[32] http://www.kingstonemedia.com/about.php, accessed January 4, 2014.

[33] Terry Lindvall, *Sanctuary Cinema: Origins of the Christian Film Industry* (New York: New York University Press, 2011), 220.

[34] http://nrb.org/about/affiliates/, accessed January 5, 2014.

[35] Ibid., 6

[36] http://www.daveyandgoliath.org/timeline.html, accessed May 7, 2014.

[37] http://www.thedeeparchives.com/featured_artist_bio.php4?id=16, accessed May 7, 2014.

[38] Ibid., 220.
http://www.raptureready.com/who/Russ_Doughten.html, accessed May 7, 2014.

[39] http://www.cbn.com/superbook/series-history.aspx, accessed May, 7, 2014.

[40] Ibid., 221
http://cloudtenpictures.com/site2/about-cloud-ten, accessed May 7, 2014.

[41] http://www.imdb.com/?ref_=nv_home, accessed May 7, 2014.

[42] http://www.lightworkersmedia.com, accessed May 7, 2014.

[43] http://www.kidwaresoftware.com/about.htm, accessed May 13, 2014.

[44] http://www.wisdomtreegames.com/games.html, accessed May 13, 2014.

Chapter Six

[1] Laurie F Maffly-Kipp, Leigh E Schmidt, and Mark Valeri, *The Practice of Dance for the Future of Christianity in Practicing Protestants: Histories of Christian Life in America 1630–1965*,(Baltimore: The Johns Hopkins University Press, 1990).

[2] Larry Eskridge, *God's Forever Family: The Jesus Movement in America* (Oxford: Oxford University Press, 2013), 92.

[3] http://www.colinharbinson.com/toymakerandson/history.html, accessed July 24, 2014.

[4] http://www.balletmagnificat.com/people/keith-thibodeaux, accessed November 29, 2013.

[5] http://www.balletmagnificat.com/people/kathy-thibodeaux, accessed November 29, 2013.

[6] http://www.balletmagnificat.com/school-of-the-arts/class-descriptions2013, accessed November 29, 2013.

[7] Ibid.

[8] http://www.balletmagnificat.com/tour-companies, accessed November 29, 2013.

[9] http://www.icdf.com/america.php, accessed November 29, 2013.

[10] http://www.icdf.com/contact-icdf-countries.php, accessed November 29, 2013.

[11] http://www.crossingsdance.com/#/about-us/our-faculty, accessed November 29, 2013.

[12] https://www.facebook.com/masterworkstouringcompany/info, accessed December 1, 2013.

[13] http://www.natldancenetwork.com/NLDNHistory.html, accessed December 1, 2013.

[14] http://www.natldancenetwork.com/NLDNHistory.html, accessed December 1, 2013.

[15] http://www.danceaddeum.com/about/director/, accessed December 1, 2013.

[16] http://www.danceaddeum.com/about/introducing-ad-deum/, accessed December 1, 2013.

[17] http://www.jubilateworshipdanceconference.com/about.html, accessed July 23, 2014

[18] http://www.projectdance.com/?page_id=161, accessed July 23, 2014.

[18] http://www.danceaddeum.com/classes/, accessed December 1, 2013.

[19] http://wordinmotion.com/about-us/directors, accessed December 27, 2013.

[20] http://www.expressionsofjoy.org/about/purpose-mission/, accessed December 29, 2013.

[21] http://www.expressionsofjoy.org/school/company/, accessed December 29, 2013.

²²http://omusa.org/dancelink/, accessed July 24, 2014.

²³ http://www.paradosiballetcompany.com/#/about-us, accessed December 27, 2013.

²⁴ http://ballet58.org, accessed December 28, 2013.

Chapter Seven
¹ http://divinity.duke.edu/initiatives-centers/dita, accessed March 18, 2014.

² Ibid.

³ http://www.dspt.edu/site/Default.aspx?PageID=147, accessed March 19, 2014.

⁴ http://www.brehmcenter.com/education/brehm_emphasis, accessed March 20, 2014.

⁵ http://gtu.edu/academics/areas/art-religion, accessed March 20, 2014.

⁶ http://www.regent-college.edu/graduate-programs/mats, accessed March 21, 2014.

⁷ http://www.regent-college.edu/our-campus/art-and-architecture, accessed March 21, 2014.

⁸ http://www.regent-college.edu/our-campus/lookout-gallery, accessed March 21, 2014.

⁹ http://www.st-andrews.ac.uk/itia/seminar.html, accessed March 21, 2014.

¹⁰ http://ism.yale.edu, accessed March 21, 2014.

¹¹ http://ism.yale.edu/academic-life/graduate-study/ism-and-yale-divinity-school, accessed March 21, 2014.

¹² http://www.sbts.edu/phd/prospective-students/doctor-of-philosophy/program-concentrations/christianity-and-the-arts/, accessed March 21, 2014.

¹³ http://www.sbts.edu/phd/prospective-students/doctor-of-philosophy/program-concentrations/christianity-and-the-arts/, accessed March 21, 2014.

¹⁴http://www.wesleyseminary.edu/Portals/0/Documents/Registrar/Curriculum%20Design%20for%20MA%20and%20Certificate%20in%20Theology%20and%20the%20Arts.pdf, accessed March 21, 2014.

¹⁵ Ibid.

¹⁶ http://dnn6.wesleyseminary.edu/LCAR/Community/AboutTheCenter, accessed March 21, 2014.

Chapter Eight
¹ https://columbiabaptist.org/cifa, accessed March 24, 2014.

² https://columbiabaptist.org/cifafall, accessed March 24, 2014.

³ https://columbiabaptist.org/cifa, accessed March 24, 2014.

⁴ http://www.st.lukes.org/ministries/sofa/, accessed March 25, 2014.

⁵ Ibid.

⁶ Ibid.
⁷ http://www.st.lukes.org/ministries/sofa/, accessed March 25, 2014.

⁸ http://carmellutheran.org/media/uploaded/f/0e3002515_1395070486_faa14brochure-forweb.pdf, accessed March 26, 2014.

⁹ http://www.bfmmm.com/page.aspx?page_id=54, accessed March 28, 2014.

¹⁰ http://newantiochcogic.org/?page_id=45, accessed March 28, 2014.

¹¹ http://www.stjohnokc.org/ministries/fa, accessed March 28, 2014.

¹² Ibid.

¹³ http://www.fpclakeland.org/worship/fine-arts/, accessed March 25, 2014.

¹⁴ http://www.jwumc.org/ministries/adults/music--fine-arts, accessed March 25, 2014.

¹⁵ http://journeychurch.tv/connect/creative-journey, accessed July 24, 2014.

¹⁶ http://www.blue-ridge.org/events/serve, accessed July 24, 2014.

¹⁷ http://www.johnsonferry.org/gallery.aspx, accessed March 25, 2014.

¹⁸ http://www.hohchurch.org/cloister-art-gallery, accessed March 25, 2014.

¹⁹ http://www.theevergreenchurch.org/content/view/47/53, accessed March 25, 2014.

²⁰ http://www.firstchurchdallas.org/get-involved/music-arts/goodrich-gallery/, accessed March 27, 2014.

²¹ http://www.unilu.org/gallery/past.htm, accessed March 26, 2014.

²² http://www.plymouth-church.net/art-gallery.html, accessed March 26, 2014.

²³ http://www.secondcrcgrandhaven.org/atriumartgallery.html, accessed March 26, 2014.

²⁴ http://www.graceinfo.org/events/art/previous/39-art-previous-exhibits/56-harper-leich-art-show-july-29-august-2-2012, accessed March 27, 2014.

²⁵ http://www.westpres.org/in_art_and_music/fine_arts_series_schedule.php, accessed March 27, 2014.

²⁶ http://firstsrq.com/music/fine-arts-series/, accessed March 26, 2014.

[27] http://www.stpaulucc.org/2011-11-04-20-39-21/2011-11-08-13-21-07/fine-arts-schedule.html, accessed March 26, 2014.

[28] http://stritaparish.net/index.cfm?load=page&page=80, accessed March 26, 2014.

[29] http://www.mountolivechurch.org/musicarts_musicfinearts.html, accessed March 26, 2014.

[30] http://ag.org/top/index.cfm, accessed March 26, 2014.

[31] http://music.ag.org, accessed March 26, 2014.

[32] http://faf.ag.org, accessed March 26, 2014.

[33] http://www.evangel.edu/academics/undergraduate/programs-list/, accessed March 26, 2014.

[34] https://hillsong.com/en/, accessed March 30, 2014.

[35] http://hillsongcollege.com/streams-courses/ministry/certiv, accessed March 30, 2014.

[36] http://www.presbyterianmission.org/ministries/arts/, accessed March 30, 2014.

[37] http://www.presbymusic.org/about.html, accessed March 30, 2014.

[38] http://www.belhaven.edu/academics/divisions.htm, accessed March 30, 2014.

[39] http://saddleback.com/connect/ministries, accessed March 30, 2014.

[40] http://saddleback.com/connect/ministry/ex-creatis-arts/lake-forest, accessed March 30, 2014.

[41] http://www.lifeway.com/Article/news-sbc-baptisms-churches-increased-in-2011-membership-declined, accessed March 30, 2014.

[42] http://www.baptistschools.org/member-schools/, accessed March 30, 2014.

[43] http://www.liberty.edu/academics/communications/coms/index.cfm?PID=104, accessed March 30, 2014.

[44] http://www.liberty.edu/academics/music/index.cfm?PID=28625, accessed March 30, 2014.

[45] http://www.willowcreek.org/aboutwillow/what-willow-believes, accessed March 31, 2014.

[46] Ibid.

Chapter Nine

[1] http://www.crossrhythms.co.uk/articles/music/The_Continental_Singers_Over_60_albums_over_1500_concerts_a_year/34680/p1/, accessed February 13, 2014.

[2] http://www.crossrhythms.co.uk/articles/music/The_Continental_Singers_Over_60_albums_over_1500_concerts_a_year/34680/p1/, accessed February 14, 2014.

[3] http://www.christianartists.org/node/114, accessed February 14, 2014.

[4] http://www.christianartists-network.org/what-is-and-does-christian-artists/, accessed February 14, 2014.

[5] http://www.christianartists-network.org/members/, accessed February 14, 2014.

[6] http://actinternational.org/about_act_history.aspx, accessed February 14, 2014.

[7] http://actinternational.org/about_act_history.aspx, accessed February 14, 2014.

[8] http://iamencounter.com/e11/?p=152, accessed February 14, 2014.

[9] http://www.artscentregroup.org.uk/about.php, accessed February 14, 2014.

[10] http://www.artscentregroup.org.uk/patrons.php, accessed February 14, 2014.

[11] http://www.icdf.com/icdf-history.php, accessed February 14, 2014.

[12] http://www.icdf.com/icdf-networks-up-close.php, accessed February 14, 2014.

[13] http://www.icdf.com/icdf-dance-ministry-courses.php, accessed February 14, 2014.

[14] http://www.icdf.com/national-cdfs.php, accessed February 14, 2014.

[15] http://www.ywamcas.org/opportunities/schools, accessed February 25, 2014.

[16] http://acetrust.org/about-ace, accessed February 21, 2014.

[17] http://www.creativeartseurope.org/Creative_Arts_Europe/The_CAE_Story.html, accessed February 21, 2014.

[18] http://www.vatican.va/news_services/press/documentazione/documents/santopadre_biografie/giovanni_paolo_ii_biografia_breve_en.html, accessed June 2, 2014.

[19] http://www.vatican.va/holy_father/john_paul_ii/letters/documents/hf_jp-ii_let_23041999_artists_en.html, accessed June 2, 2014.

[20] Ibid.

[21] http://www.vatican.va/holy_father/john_paul_ii/letters/documents/hf_jp-ii_let_23041999_artists_en.html, accessed June 2, 2014.

[22] http://www.worldofworship.org/vision.php, accessed June 2, 2014.

[23] http://www.worldofworship.org/heartmusic.php, accessed June 2, 2014.

[24] http://www.worldofworship.org/board.php, accessed July 17, 2014.

[25] http://www.arts.om.org, accessed February 21, 2014.

[26] http://www.arts.om.org, accessed February 21, 2014.

[27] Ibid.

[28] http://news.om.org/country-article/r39891, accessed February 21, 2014.

[29] http://www.lausanne.org/en/documents/lausanne-covenant.html, accessed February 21, 2014.

[30] http://www.lausanne.org/docs/2004forum/LOP46_IG17.pdf, accessed February 22, 2014.

[31] Ibid.

[32] http://www.lausanne.org/en/about/faqs.html

[33] http://www.lausanne.org/en/documents/ctcommitment.html, accessed February 23, 2014.

[34] http://www.lausanne.org/en/documents/ctcommitment.html, accessed February 23, 2014.

[35] http://www.lausanne.org/en/documents/ctcommitment/bibliographic-resources.html, accessed February 24, 2014.

[36] http://www.worldea.org/news/3718/Arts-in-Mission-2011-Press-Release, accessed February 24, 2014.

[37] Ibid.

[38] http://www.lausanne.org/en/about/news-releases/1864-lausanne-movement-appoints-senior-associate-for-the-arts.html, accessed February 24, 2014.

BIBLIOGRAPHY

Acacia Theatre Company. "About Acacia." http://www.acaciatheatre.com/about.php.

Ad Deum Dance Company. "Director Randall Flinn." http://www.danceaddeum.com/about/director/.

A.D. Players. "Leadership." http://adplayers.org/leadership.html.

Alfonso, Barry. *The Billboard Guide to Contemporary Christian Music*. New York: Billboard Books, 2002.

Alliance of Confessing Evangelicals, Inc. "Gene Veith." http://www.alliancenet.org/CC/article/0,,PTID307086_CHID564292_CIID1414980,00.html.

All of Life Redeemed. "Seerveld Pages." http://www.allofliferedeemed.co.uk/seerveld.htm.

Art and Christian Enquiry. "About ACE." http://acetrust.org/about-ace.

Arts Centre Group. "About Us." http://www.artscentregroup.org.uk/about.php.

Arts Centre Group. "Patrons." http://www.artscentregroup.org.uk/patrons.php.

Artists in Christian Testimony International. "History of Artists in Christian Testimony International." http://actinternational.org/about_act_history.aspx.

Bahamas Faith Ministries International Fellowship. "BFMI Worship Fine Arts
	Department." http://www.bfmmm.com/page.aspx?page_id=54.

Baker, Paul. *Contemporary Christian Music: Where It Came From, Where It Is,
	Where It Is Going.* Westchester: Crossway Books, 1985. Accessed February 6,
	2014. http://www.ccel.us/CCM.ch2.html.

Baker, Paul. *Contemporary Christian Music: Where It Came From, Where It Is,
	Where It Is Going.* Westchester: Crossway Books, 1985. Accessed January 25,
	2014. http://www.ccel.us/CCM.ch12.html.

Baker, Paul. *Contemporary Christian Music: Where It Came From, Where It Is,
	Where It Is Going.* Westchester: Crossway Books, 1985. Accessed January 26,
	2014. http://www.ccel.us/CCM.ch3.html.

Ballet 5:8. "Home." http://ballet58.org.

Ballet Magnificat! "The People of Ballet Magnificat! Keith Thibodeaux."
	http://www.balletmagnificat.com/people/keith-thibodeaux.

Belhaven University. "Academics."
	http://www.belhaven.edu/academics/divisions.htm.

Blue Ridge Community Church. "Serve." http://www.blue-ridge.org/events/serve.

Brehm Center. "Education."
	http://www.brehmcenter.com/education/brehm_emphasis.

Butler, Nate. "Christian Comics Pioneers." *Comix 35.* Accessed January 3, 2014
	http://www.christiancomicsinternational.org/pioneers1.html#Anchor-
	FRANK-49575.

Candler, Martha. *Drama in Religious Service.* New York: New Century Co., 1922.
	http://www.archive.org/stream/cu31924026102875#page/n13/mode/
	2up.

Carmel Lutheran Church. "Carmel Lutheran Church Fine Arts Academy."
	http://carmellutheran.org/media/uploaded/f/0e3002515_1395070486_faa
	14brochure-forweb.pdf.

Catholic Artists Society. "Mass of the Holy Spirit for Artists."
	http://www.catholicartistssociety.org/2011/04/.

Chang, Pauline J. "Methodists Celebrate Music Past, Present and Future." *The
	Christian Post*, July 21, 2005. Accessed September 23, 2013.
	http://www.christianpost.com/news/methodists-celebrate-music-past-
	present-and-future-3738/.

Christian Artists Europe. "Members."
	http://www.christianartists-network.org/members/.

Christian Artists Europe. "What is and does Christian Artists?"

Christian Artists Seminar Europe. "History." http://www.christianartists.org/node/114. Christian Artists Seminar. "Staff." http://christianartistsseminars.com/staff/. http://www.christianartists-network.org/what-is-and-does-christian-artists/.

Christian Broadcasting Network. "Superbook Series History." http://www.cbn.com/superbook/series-history.aspx.

Christian Festival Association. "About Us." http://bobthompson121.wix.com/cfa-sponsorship#!about-us/csgz.

Christians in the Theatre Arts. "CITA Home/" http://cita.org/site/.

Christians in the Visual Arts. "CIVA Publications." http://civa.org/resources/civa-publications/.

Christian Youth Theater- San Diego. "About CYT." http://www.cytsandiego.org/about/.

Cloud Ten Pictures. "About Cloud Ten Pictures." http://cloudtenpictures.com/site2/about-cloud-ten.

Columbia Baptist Church. "Columbia Institute of Fine Arts." https://columbiabaptist.org/cifa.

Covenant Players. "Mission and Doctrine." http://covenantplayers.org/mission-and-doctrine.

Cram, Ralph Adams. *The Ministry of Art*. Boston: Houghton Mifflin Company, 1914. http://www.archive.org/stream/ministryofart00cramiala#page/viii/mode/2up.

Creation Festival. "The Creation History." http://creationfest.com/nw/about-us/story/.

Creative Arts Europe. "The CAE Story." http://www.creativeartseurope.org/

Creative Arts Europe/The_CAE_Story.html.

Crossings Dance Ministries. "About Us." http://www.crossingsdance.com/#/about-us/our-faculty.

Cross Rhythms. "The Continental Singers: Over 60 albums, over 1,500 concerts a year. *Cross Rhythms*, December 24, 2008. Accessed February 13, 2014. http://www.crossrhythms.co.uk/articles/music/The_Continental_Singers_Over_60_albums_over_1500_concerts_a_year/34680/p1/.

Crumm, David. "Zondervan Publishes Comic Book Revelation." *Read the Spirit*, Accessed January 4, 2014. http://www.readthespirit.com/explore/zondervan-publishes-comic-book-revelation/.

Darlene Zschech. "Biography." http://www.darlenezschech.com/biography/.

Davis, D. Jack, Margo DeHoyas, Autumn Lopez, Rachael Garnett, Stacie Gower, Amanda Sayle, Neil Sreenan, et al. "History of Art Education." http://art.unt.edu/ntieva/HistoryofArtEd/1901-events.html.

Dominion School of Philosophy and Theology. "Home." http://www.dspt.edu/site/Default.aspx?PageID=147.

Duke Divinity School. "Initiatives and Centers: Initiatives in Theology and the Arts." http://divinity.duke.edu/initiatives-centers/dita/director.

Eskridge, Larry. "Christian History: The "Praise and Worship" Revolution." *Christianity Today*. October 29, 2008. Accessed April 29, 2014. http://www.christianitytoday.com/ch/thepastinthepresent/storybehind/praiseworshiprevolution.html?start=2.

Eskridge, Larry. *Gods Forever Family*. Oxford: Oxford University Press, 2013.

Evangelical Lutheran Church in America. *Davey and Goliath*. http://www.daveyandgoliath.org/timeline.html.

Evangel University. "Undergraduate Programs." http://www.evangel.edu/academics/undergraduate/programs-list/.

Expressions of Joy. "Vision and Mission." http://www.expressionsofjoy.org/about/purpose-mission/.

Facebook. "Master Works Touring Company. https://www.facebook.com/masterworkstouringcompany/info.

Fawcett, Cheryl L., and Thompson, Jamie. "Frank E. Gabelein." Talbot School of Theology, Biola University (website). http://www.talbot.edu/ce20/educators/protestant/frank_gaebelein/.

First Presbyterian Church. "Fine Arts Ministries." http://www.fpclakeland.org/worship/fine-arts/.

First United Methodist Church. "Goodrich Gallery." http://www.firstchurchdallas.org/get-involved/music-arts/goodrich-gallery/.

First United Methodist Church. "Music Fine Arts Series." http://firstsrq.com/music/fine-arts-series/.

Gaither Music. "Bill Gaither." http://gaither.com/artists/bill-gaither.

Galli, Mark. "Dorothy Sayers: Mystery writer and apologist." August 8, 2008. http://www.ctlibrary.com/ch/131christians/musiciansartistsandwriters/sayers.html.

Galli, Mark. "Fanny Crosby: Prolific and blind writer." August 8, 2008.
http://www.christianitytoday.com/ch/131christians/poets/crosby.html?start=2.

Gehring, Charles. "Nicholas Wolterstorff (1932): Academic/Scholar." New Netherlands Institute. http://www.newnetherlandinstitute.org/history-and-heritage/dutch_americans/nicholas-wolterstorff/.

Goff, James R. *Close Harmony: A History of Southern Gospel.* Chapel Hill: University of North Carolina Press, 2002.

Gospel Music Hall of Fame. "Charles A. Tindley." http://www.gmahalloffame.org/speaker-lineup/charles-a-tindley/.

Gospel Music Workshop of America. "History." http://gmwanational.net/History.htm.

Gospel Music Workshop of America. "Reverend James Cleveland." http://gmwanational.net/about-gmwa/reverend-james-cleveland/.

Grace Community Church. "Grace Centre Art Gallery." http://www.graceinfo.org/events/art/previous/39-art-previous-exhibits/56-harper-leich-art-show-july-29-august-2-2012.

Graduate Theological Union. "Academics." http://gtu.edu/academics/areas/art-religion.

Haney, James Parton, ed. *Art Education in the Public Schools of the United States.* New York: American Art Annual Incorporated, 1908. http://www.archive.org/stream/arteducationinpu00haneiala#page/270/mode/2up.

Harbinson, Colin. "About Colin Harbinson." http://www.colinharbinson.com/bio/index.html.

Henry Luce III Center for the Arts and Religion. "About the Center." http://dnn6.wesleyseminary.edu/LCAR/Community/AboutTheCenter.

Hildreth Meiere. "Profile." http://www.hildrethmeiere.com/Profile.html.

Hill, Ian. *New Georgia Encyclopedia.* "'Georgia Tom' Dorsey (1899-1993)." Atlanta: New Georgia Encyclopedia, 2014. http://www.georgiaencyclopedia.org/articles/arts-culture/georgia-tom-dorsey-1899-1993.

Hillsong Church. "College." https://hillsong.com/en/.

Hillsong Church. "Courses." http://hillsongcollege.com/streams-courses/ministry/certiv.

"Ichthus music festival to return in 2014 at Kentucky Horse Park." *The Jessamine Journal,* May 8, 2013. Accessed January 21, 2014.

http://www.centralkynews.com/jessaminejournal/news/ichthus-music-festival-to-return-in-at-kentucky-horse-park/article_7da52098-9f28-5266-a85e-af62aaa70dd8.html.

International Fine Print Dealers Association. "Henry Turner Bailey." http://www.ifpda.org/content/node/172.

Internet Movie Database. "Sherwood Pictures." http://www.imdb.com/?ref_=nv_home.

Institute of Sacred Music. "Institute of Sacred Music." http://ism.yale.edu.

Institute for Theology, Imagination and the Arts. "Weekly Postgraduate Seminar." http://www.st-andrews.ac.uk/itia/seminar.html.

International Arts Movement. "Nigel Goodwin." http://iamencounter.com/e11/?p=152.

International Association of Baptist Colleges and Universities. "Member Schools." http://www.baptistschools.org/member-schools/.

International Christian Dance Fellowship. "Americas." http://www.icdf.com/america.php.

International Christian Dance Fellowship. "ICDF Dance Ministry Courses." http://www.icdf.com/icdf-dance-ministry-courses.php.

International Christian Dance Fellowship. "ICDF History." http://www.icdf.com/icdf-history.php.

International Christian Dance Fellowship. "ICDF Networks Up Close." http://www.icdf.com/icdf-networks-up-close.php.

International Christian Dance Fellowship. "National CDFs." http://www.icdf.com/national-cdfs.php.

International Council of Ethnodoxologists. "Heart Music." http://www.worldofworship.org/heartmusic.php.

International Council of Ethnodoxologists. "Vision Statement of ICE." http://www.worldofworship.org/vision.php.

Johnson Ferry Baptist Church. "Glimpses of His Glorty Gallery." http://www.johnsonferry.org/gallery.aspx.

John Wesley United Methodist Church. "Music and Fine Arts." http://www.jwumc.org/ministries/adults/music--fine-arts.

JourneyChurch.tv. "Creative Journey." http://journeychurch.tv/connect/creative-journey.

Kempster, James J., ed. *Union Now*. New York: Union Theological Seminary, 2010. http://www.utsnyc.edu/document.doc?id=548.

Kidware Software. "About Kidware Software, LLC. http://www.kidwaresoftware.com/about.htm.

Kingstone Media. "Bible Comics." http://www.kingstonemedia.com/biblecomics.php

Kirk Franklin. "Biography." http://www.kirkfranklin.com/biography.

Kuyper, Abraham. *Six Stone Lectures*. Princeton, 1898. https://archive.org/details/calvinismsixst00kuyp.

L'Abri Fellowship International. "L'Abri Fellowship History." http://www.labri.org/history.html.

Lamb's Players Theatre. "About Lamb's." http://www.lambsplayers.org/about.php.

Larry Norman. "Larry Norman: 1947-2008." http://www.larrynorman.com.

Liberty University. "Communication." http://www.liberty.edu/academics/communications/coms/index.cfm?PID=104.

Liberty University. "Music." http://www.liberty.edu/academics/music/index.cfm?PID=28625

Liberty University. "Students Join 40th Year of TRBC Christmas Show" http://www.liberty.edu/news/?PID=18495&MID=24579.

Lifeway Christian Resources. "SBC Baptisms and Churches Increased in 2011, Membership Declined." *Lifeway*, June 12, 2012. Accessed March 30, 2014. http://www.lifeway.com/Article/news-sbc-baptisms-churches-increased-in-2011-membership-declined

LightWorkers Media. "About." http://www.lightworkersmedia.com.

LightWorkers Media. "The Bible Series." http://www.bibleseries.tv/about/.

Lindvall, Terry. *Sanctuary Cinema: Origins of the Christian Film Industry*. New York: New York University Press, 2011.

MacFarland, Charles S. *The Churches of the Federal Council*. New York: Fleming H. Revell Company, 1916. http://www.archive.org/stream/churchesoffedera00macf#page/n7/mode/2up.

Maffly-Kipp, Laurie F., Schmidt, Leigh E., and Valeri, Mark. *Practicing Protestants: Histories of Christian Life in America, 1630-1965*. Baltimore: John Hopkins University Press, 2006.

Magee, Harriet Cecil. *Where to go and what to see: a short history of art*. Boston: The Christopher Publishing House, 1932. http://openlibrary.org/works/OL7793914W/Where_to_go_and_what_to_see.

Makoto Fujimura. "Fujimura Institute." http://fujimurainstitute.org.

Makoto Fujimura. "International Arts Movement." http://www.internationalartsmovement.org.

Makoto Fujimura. "Makoto Fujimura Bio." http://www.makotofujimura.com/bio/.

Maranatha! Music. "About Maranatha! Music." http://www.maranathamusic.com/about/.

Masterworks Festival. "The Christian Performing Artists' Fellowship Vision." http://www.masterworksfestival.org/vision.html.

McNeil, W.K. *Encyclopedia of American Gospel Music*. New York: Routledge, Taylor & Francis Group, 2005. http://books.google.com/books?id=uqT-CJYcqskC&printsec=frontcover&source=gbs_ge_summary_r&cad=0#v=onepage&q&f=false.

Michael W. Smith. "Biography." http://www.michaelwsmith.com/bio.html.

Miller, Madeleine Sweeny. *Church Pageantry*. New York: Methodist Book Concern, 1924. http://www.archive.org/stream/MN41748ucmf_3#page/n31/mode/2up.

Mind Garage. "First Live Christian Rock Worship Service in the World." http://mindgarage.com/emass1.html.

Mind Garage. "The Village Voice." http://www.mindgarage.com/voice.html.

Mount Olive Lutheran Church. "Music and Fine Arts Series." http://www.mountolivechurch.org/musicarts_musicfinearts.html.

Nashville Songwriters Foundation. "Thomas A. Dorsey." http://www.nashvillesongwritersfoundation.com/d-g/thomas-a-dorsey.aspx.

National Association of Pastoral Musicians. http://www.npm.org/main/current.html.

National Convention of Gospel Choirs and Choruses. "Beginnings of NCGCC." http://www.ncgccinc.com/new/index.php/history/beginnings

National Council of Churches. "About the National Council of Churches." http://www.nationalcouncilofchurches.us/about/

National Religious Broadcasters. "NRB Affiliates." http://nrb.org/about/affiliates/.

Neill, Steve. "Priests Celebrate 50th Anniversary: Father Virgil C. Funk." May 27, 2013. http://www.catholicvirginian.org/archive/2013/2013vol88iss15/pages/profile.html.

NetHymnal. "Ira David Sankey:1840-1908."
    http://www.cyberhymnal.org/bio/s/a/n/sankey_id.htm.

NetHymnal. "William Fiske Sherman:1826-1888."
    http://www.cyberhymnal.org/bio/s/h/e/sherwin_wf.htm.

New Antioch Church of God in Christ. "Drama and Fine Arts Department."
    http://newantiochcogic.org/?page_id=45.

Night of Miracles. "A Journey to Bethlehem." http://www.thenightofmiracles.com.

Noland, Rory. "About Rory." http://www.heartoftheartist.org/about-rory/.

Operation Mobilization International. "Incarnate School of Art and Mission 2014 Begins." *OM International News*, February 13, 2014. Accessed February 21, 2014. http://news.om.org/country-article/r39891.

Operation Mobilization Arts International. "Welcome." http://www.arts.om.org.

Paradosi Ballet Company. "About Us."
    http://www.paradosiballetcompany.com/#/about-us.

Passion Conferences. "268 Declaration."
    http://www.268generation.com/#!declaration.

Plymouth Congregational Church. "Plymouth Art Gallery." http://www.plymouth-church.net/art-gallery.html.

Premier Festivals. "About Us." http://www.premierfestivals.com/about.

Presbyterian Historical Society. "Guides to Archival Collections."
    http://history.pcusa.org/collections/research-tools/guides-archival-collections?record_id=NCC6.

Presbyterian Church (USA). "Presbyterian Association of Musicians."
    http://www.presbymusic.org/about.html.

Presbyterian Church (USA). "Worship and the Arts."
    http://www.presbyterianmission.org/ministries/arts/.

Price, Jay M. *Temples for a Modern God*. Oxford: Oxford University Press, 2013.

Project Dance. "About Us ." http://www.projectdance.com/?page_id=1212#

Ralph Carmichael. "Big Band." http://www.ralphcarmichael.com/bigband.php.

Regent College. "Graduate Programs." http://www.regent-college.edu/graduate-programs/mats.

Roberts, Preston. "The Field of Religion and Art at Chicago," *The Christian Scholar* 40, no. 4(1957): 339– 345. Accessed September 22, 2013. http://www.jstor.org/discover/10.2307/41177043?uid=3739936&uid=2134&uid=2&uid=70&uid=4&uid= 3739256&sid=21102648293191.

Rock and Roll Hall of Fame. "Mahalia Jackson." https://rockhall.com/inductees/mahalia-jackson/timeline/

Saddleback Church. "Connect." http://saddleback.com/connect/ministries.

Saddleback Church. "Ex Creatis Arts Initiative." http://saddleback.com/connect/ministry/ex-creatis-arts/lake-forest.

Sanford, Benjamin Elias, ed. *Church federation, Inter-church conference on federation*. New York: Fleming H. Revell Company, 1906. http://books.google.com/books?id=UShOAAAAYAAJ&printsec=frontcover&source=gbs_ge_ summary_r&cad=0#v=onepage&q&f=false.

Schaeffer, Francis. *Art and the Bible* (Downers Grove: Intervarsity Press, 1973), 17.

Second Christian Reformed Church. "Atrium Art Gallery." http://www.secondcrcgrandhaven.org/atriumartgallery.html.

Sight and Sound Theatres. "The History of Sight and Sound Theatres." http://www.sight-sound.com/WebSite/history.do.

Smith, H. Augustine. *Worship in the Church School Through Music, Pageantry and Pictures*. Elgin: David C. Cook Publishing, 1928.

Sorensen, Lee. "Rookmaaker, Henderik Roelof 'Hans '. Dictionary of Art Historians (website). http://www.dictionaryofarthistorians.org/rookmaakerh.htm.

St. Catherine University. "Catholic Art Association Materials: The Ade Bethune Papers." http://library.stkate.edu/archives/bethune-caafa#ref69.

Steven Curtis Chapman. "About." http://stevencurtischapman.com/about/.

St. Luke's Methodist Church. "School of Fine Arts." http://www.st.lukes.org/ministries/sofa/.

St. Paul United Church of Christ. "Fine Arts Schedule." http://www.stpaulucc.org/2011-11-04-20-39-21/2011-11-08-13-21-07/fine-arts-schedule.html

Stowe, David W. *No Sympathy for the Devil*. North Carolina: University of Chapel Hill Press, 2011.

Strandburg, Todd. "Russ Doughton." *Rapture Ready*. Accessed May 7, 2014. http://www.raptureready.com/who/Russ_Doughten.html.

St Rita Catholic Community. "St. Rita Fine Arts Series." http://stritaparish.net/index.cfm?load=page&page=80.

Taylor, J. Mark. email message to the author, June 4, 2014.

The Bible In Practical life: Proceedings of the Second Annual Convention. Chicago:

Executive Office of the Association, 1904.
http://www.archive.org/stream/bibleinpractical00reli#page/484/mode/2up.

The Deep Archives. "Featured Artist Bio."
http://www.thedeeparchives.com/featured_artist_bio.php4?id=16.

The Dorothy L. Sayers Society. "Dorothy Sayers."
http://www.sayers.org.uk/dorothy.html.

The Episcopal Actors Guild of America, Inc. "More About the Episcopal Actors' Guild." http://www.actorsguild.org/aboutus2.html.

The Evergreen Church. "Art Gallery."
http://www.theevergreenchurch.org/content/view/47/53.

The General Council of the Assemblies of God. "Assemblies of God."
http://ag.org/top/index.cfm.

The General Council of the Assemblies of God. "Fine Arts." http://faf.ag.org.

The General Council of the Assemblies of God. "Worship Resource and Consulting."
http://music.ag.org.

The Gombach Group. "Living Places: Chautauqua Institution Historic District."
http://www.livingplaces.com/NY/Chautauqua_County/Chautauqua_Town/Chautauqua_Institution_Historic_District.html.

The House of Hope Presbyterian Church. Cloister Art Gallery."
http://www.hohchurch.org/cloister-art-gallery.

The Internet Archive. *The Proceedings of the First Religious Education Association.* Chicago: The Religious Education Association, 1903.
http://archive.org/stream/religiouseducati00reli#page/n5/mode/2up.

The Lausanne Movement. "Bibliographical Resources for the Cape Town Commitment. "http://www.lausanne.org/en/documents/ctcommitment/bibliographic-resources.html.

The Lausanne Movement. "Frequently Asked Questions."
http://www.lausanne.org/en/about/faqs.html.

The Lausanne Movement. "Lausanne Movement Appoints Senior Associate for the Arts." http://www.lausanne.org/en/about/news-releases/1864-lausanne-movement-appoints-senior-associate-for-the-arts.html.

The Lausanne Movement. "Redeeming the Art: The Restoration of the Arts to God's Creational Intention." Harbinson, Colin, Franklin, John, Tughan, James, Novak, Phillis, and others. Edited by David Claydon. Paper developed as part of Issue Group on Redeeming the Arts for the 2004 Forum for World Evangelization. Accessed February 23, 2014.
http://www.lausanne.org/docs/2004forum/LOP46_IG17.pdf.

The Lausanne Movement. "The Cape Town Commitment."
http://www.lausanne.org/en/documents/ctcommitment.html

The Lausanne Movement. "The Lausanne Covenant." Accessed February 21, 2014. http://www.lausanne.org/en/documents/lausanne-covenant.html.

The Liturgical Conference. http://www.liturgicalconference.org/Liturgical_Conference/Welcome.html.

The National Liturgical Dance Network. "NLCN History." http://www.natldancenetwork.com/NLDNHistory.html.

The Society for the Arts, Religion and Contemporary Culture. "Arc Fellows." http://www.sarcc.org/fellows.htm.

The Society of Catholic Artists. ""Who Are We?" http://www.catholicartists.co.uk.

The Southern Baptist Theological Seminary. "Christianity and the Arts." http://www.sbts.edu/phd/prospective-students/doctor-of-philosophy/program-concentrations/christianity-and-the-arts/.

The Vatican. "His Holiness John Paul II Short Biography Pre-Pontificate." *Holy See Press Office*, February 13, 2001. Accessed June 2, 2014. http://www.vatican.va/news_services/press/documentazione/documents/santopadre_biografie/giovanni_paolo_ii_biografia_breve_en.html.

The Vatican. "Letter of His Holiness Pope John Paul II to Artists." *Libreria Editrice Vaticana*, April 4, 1999. Accessed June 2, 2014. http://www.vatican.va/holy_father/john_paul_ii/letters/documents/hf_jp-ii_let_23041999_artists_en.html.

University Lutheran Church. "The Gallery at University Lutheran Church." http://www.unilu.org/gallery/past.htm.

Vincent, John H. *The Chautauqua Movement*. Boston, 1886. https://archive.org/stream/chautauquamovem00millgoog#page/n302/mode/2up.

Vineyard Worship. "About." http://www.vineyardworship.com/about.

Westminster Presbyterian Church. "Discovering God in Art and Music." http://www.westpres.org/in_art_and_music/fine_arts_series_schedule.php.

Wesleyan University. "Friends of the Wesleyan Library: Library Greats, Caleb Thomas Winchester." http://www.wesleyan.edu/library/friends/lib_greats.html.

Wesley Theological Seminary. "Master Degree Programs." http://www.wesleyseminary.edu/Portals/0/Documents/Registrar/Curriculum%20Design%20for%20MA%20and%20Certificate%20in%20Theology%20and%20the%20Arts.

White, Susan J. *Art, Architecture, and Liturgical Reform: The Liturgical Arts Society 1928-1972*. New York: Pueblo Publishing Company, 1990.

Willman, Chris. "Randy Stonehill Celebrates 20 Years Of Humor, Humanity, & The Hope Of Glory." *CCM Magazine*, August, 1990. Accessed January 28, 2014. http://www.nifty-music.com/stonehill/ccm0890.html.

Willow Creek Community Church. "About Willow." http://www.willowcreek.org/aboutwillow/what-willow-believes.

Wisdom Tree Games. "Games." http://www.wisdomtreegames.com/games.html.

Word In Motion Dance Company. "Directors." http://wordinmotion.com/about-us/directors.

World Evangelical Alliance. "Arts in Mission Press Release." http://www.worldea.org/news/3718/Arts-in-Mission-2011-Press-Release.

Youth with a Mission. "University of the Nations College of Arts and Sports." http://www.ywamcas.org/opportunities/schools.

INDEX

Abraham and Isaac 47
Abstract 78,79
Acacia Theatre Company 51
ACB Russia 84
A Christian Doctrine of the Arts and Religious Experience 103
Acting 28, 46, 53, 54, 91, 123
Action Bible 83
Adams, Yolanda 63
Ad Deum Dance Company 95
A.D. Players 49, 50
Aesthetic Theory 103
After-School Instruction 108
Agape 64
Agape Europe 119
AgapeFest 68
A. J. Showalter Company 59
Album 64, 55, 66, 72, 97, 117
A Letter Of His Holiness Pope John Paul II

To Artists 121
Alive Festival 68
All Nations Christian College 126
All Saved Freak Band 64
Amazing Saints 82
American Music Awards 66
Amos, Daniel 65
Andrae Crouch and the Disciples 63, 64
Andrews Gospel Singers 62
Angelic Gospel Singers 62
Angelicum 101
Animation 70, 85
Architecture .... 26, 27, 28, 30, 70, 74, ...75, 76, 77, 100, 101
Aretha Franklin 62
Art and Christianity 120
Art and Christianity Enquiry Trust 120
Art House 117
Artist Development 111

Artistic Director 98
Artists in Christian Testimony
International 30, 115, 123, 126
Artist-in-Residence 124
Arts Administration 113
Arts Centre Group 119
Arts Director 106
*Arts in Mission: Training for
Cross-Cultural Ministry* 123
Artslink 124
Arts Ministry 53, 104, 107, 113, 118, 123
Arts Outreach 113, 121
Art-Theology-Church
International Conference 120
Association of Christian Media
Southern Africa 84
Athens Music Company 59
AtlantaFest 68
Atrium Art Gallery 111
Audio 87, 109
Audio Streaming 109
Avatar 87
Ayris, Art 83
"Baby, Baby" 65, 80
Bailey, Henry Turner 25, 26, 73
Ballet 10, 70, 92, 93, 94, 95, 97, 98, 107
Ballet 5:8 98
Ballet Magnificat! 10, 92, 93, 95
Barr, Alfred 29, 78
Bates, C.L. 47
Baxter, Jesse Randall Jr. 59
Beach Blast 67
Beard, Frank 13, 81
Beard, Harrington 25
Beauty 18, 26, 77, 122, 100, 124, 125

Begbie, Jeremy 33, 100, 103
Belhaven University 95, 113
Ben Israel Ben Israel 82
Bentley, Walter 46
Berry, James 58
Bethel College 50, 79
Bethlehem 53, 65
Bethune, Ade 28
Bible Adventures 86
BibleBytes 86
Bible in the Arts 101
Bible Man 86
Bible Plays 47
Bible Scrabble Games 47
Bible Stories in Pictures 82
Bible Study through Educational Drama 47
Biblical Dramas 47
Biblical Paintings 79
Big Band 63
Big Idea Productions 85
Big Ticket Festival 68
Bill Drake Band 124
Billy Graham Evangelistic Association 82, 84
Billy Graham Presents 82
Birdsall, Douglas S. 126
Blackfriars Gallery 101
Blackwood Brothers Quartet 60
Blind Boys of Alabama 62
Bliss, Phillip Paul 14
Blogs 87
Bloodgood 65
Blue Ridge Community Church 110
Blues 61, 64, 65
Bookmaking 108
Boone, Pat 63, 67

Boston University, Department of Fine Arts in Religious Education 47
Born Twice 64
Brainwashed 64
Breuer, Marcel 78
Bride 52, 65
Brother Cajetan 75
Buckton, A.M. 47
Bureau of Church Buildings and Architecture 76
Burlap to Cashmere 67
Burnett, Mark 86
Burroughs, R.E. 75
Byers, Ruth 85
Byrne, Barry 78
Cady, J. Cleveland 23, 26
Call to Worship 113
Calvin College 31, 79
Camp Meetings 15, 17, 60, 67, 90
Campus Crusade For Christ 118, 119
Candler, Martha 43, 45, 47
Cantatas 9, 112
Cantorei 112
Cards 80
Cariello. Sergio 83
Carmichael, Ralph 48, 55, 63, 64
Carter, Fred 82
Cartooning 108
Cartoons 70, 80, 81, 82
Carver, Tennille 97
Carver, Joel 97
Catechumen 86
Cathedral 77, 120
Cathedral Quartet 60
Catholic 18-19, 28, 53, 64, 68, 75-78, 80, 101, 111
Catholic Art Association 28
Catholic Artists Society 77

Catholic Art Quarterly 28
CCM 65
Cello 107
Centenary Celebration 44
Central Music Company 59
Certificate in Theology and the Arts 101, 104
Chagall, Marc 78
Chamber Music 70, 107, 120
Chamber Music Ensemble 107
Chancel Choir 109
Chapman, Steven Curtis 66
Charismatic Movement 91, 116
Charlot, Jean 78
Chat Room 87
Chautauqua 12, 13, 14, 15, 22, 25, 81, 91
Chautauqua Society of Fine Arts 13
Chalk Talk Artist 13, 81
Children of the Day 50, 65
Choir Director 29, 47, 61, 117
Choral Conducting 70, 120
Christian Artists Seminar 67, 117
Christian Broadcasting Network 52, 85
Christian Cartoons 81, 82
Christian Comic Arts Society 82, 83
Christian Community Theater 51
Christian Dance Fellowship of America 93
Christian Dance Fellowship of Australia 93
Christian Festivals Association 68
Christian Iconography 101
Christian Media Australia 84
Christian Music Day 68
Christian Rock 9, 64, 65, 67, 92
Christians in the Theatre Arts 10, 52
Christians in the Visual Arts 10, 79
Christian Youth Theater 51
Christmas Concert 111

Chuck Wagon Gang 60
Church Architectural Guild of America 76
Church Art Gallery 110
Church of the Transfiguration 46, 90
Church Symbolism 75
Chorus 61, 117
Chroma Quartet 111
Cinematic Arts 114
CIVA Sourcebook 79
CIVA Views 79
Classical 69, 94, 97, 120
Classical Ballet 94, 97
Classical Performing Artists Fellowship 69
Clergy 30, 103
Cleveland, James 61
Clothing Embellishment 108
Cloud Ten Pictures 85
COICOM 84
Collage 108, 110
Colonial Revival 74, 76
Combs, William E. 59
Comic Book 81, 82, 83
Comic Book Artist 81, 82, 83
COMIX35 .... 35, 83
Committee on Church Architecture,
Lutheran Church, Missouri Synod 75
Communication 19, 48, 112, 122
Community Carol Sing 111
Community Chorales 111
Composer 14, 61, 117, 119
Computer Games 86
Concert 10, 13, 26, 36, 60,
...................................66, 67, 101, 103, 104, 111, 117
Conover, Elbert 75, 76
Conrod, Phillip 66, 67
Contemporary 30, 32, 48, 52, 60, 63,
....64, 65, 66, 67, 68, 78, 79
Contemporary Christian Music 60, 63, 64- 67
Contemporary Worship 68
Continental Encores 117
Continental Kids 117
Continental Orchestra 117
Converse, Florence 47
Corps Bara Dance Guild 91
Corps Bara Dance Theatre 91
Cosmics 79
Costume Design 51
Courageous 32, 83
Covenant Players 46
Cram, Ralph Adams 18, 23, 24, 26, 72
Creation Festival 64, 65
Creative Arts Europe 121
Creative Arts Pastor 106
Creative Writing 108
Crescendo 120, 121
Crosby, Fannie 13
Crossings Dance Ministries 94
Crossroads Christian Communications 85
Crouch, Andrae 63
Crouch, Paul 85
Crowder, David 69
Crowther, James E. 44
Cultural Programs 121
Curtis Institute of Music 108
Dadian Gallery 101
Dallas Holmes and Praise 62
Dancing in the Spirit 87, 88, 120
Dancelink 97, 124
Dance Performance 98
Davey and Goliath 85
David and the Giants 65, 92
David C. Cook Publishing Company 82, 83

DC Talk 66, 67
DeGarmo and Key 65
Denominations 10, 44, 45, 46, 50, 71, 75, 106
    American Baptist
    Assemblies of God
    Baptist
    Catholic
    Church of God in Christ
    Congregational
    Cumberland Presbyterian
    Disciples
    Evangelical Association
    Free Will Baptist
    Friends
    Lutheran
    Methodist Church
    Methodist-Episcopal
    Methodist Episcopal South
    Pentecostal Holiness
    Presbyterian
    Protestant Episcopal
    Reformed Episcopal
    Southern Baptist
    United Brethren
    United Presbyterian
    United Methodist Church
    Wesleyan Methodist
Department of Architecture,
Southern Baptist Church 72, 73
Department of Missionary Education of the
Baptist Board of Education 42
Department of Missions of Protestant
Episcopal Church 42
Department of Worship and the Arts, National
Council of Churches 26, 45
Digital Arts 110, 111
Digital Media and Communication Arts 111
Dinner Theatre 103
Duffield, Howard 22
Doctorate of Philosophy in Art and Religion 101
Doctor of Philosophy in Christianity
and the Arts 103
Doctorate of Philosophy in Theology, Art,
Culture, and Worship 101
Doctor of Theology 98
Doctor of Theology in Theology, Imagination,
and the Arts 103
Dominican School of Philosophy
and Theology 101
Dooyeweerd, Herman 27
Dorsey, Thomas Andrew 14, 60, 61, 62
Doughten, Russ 85
Dove Awards 63
Downey, Roma 86
Drama in Religious Service 47
Drama Ministry 109
Drawings 99
Duke Divinity School 33, 100
Duke Initiative in Theology
and the Arts 33, 100
East to West Festival 68
Electric Liturgy 61
Elevate Festival 65
"El Shaddai" 65
"Emmanuel" 65
Enrich 114
Entertainment 86
Episcopal Actors Guild 45
Epworth League of the Methodist
Episcopal Church 45
Eshelman, Glen 47
Ethnomusicology 103

Euphonium 107
Evangelical Movement 15, 90
Evangelism 83, 86, 118, 124, 127
Evergreen Art Gallery 110
Ex Creatis Arts 113
Exhibit 9, 22, 30, 40, 75, 79,
.... 98, 101, 110, 111, 113
Exhibition 28, 29, 33, 103, 112, 120, 121
Exodus 86
Explo '72 67
Expressions of Joy 97
Facing the Giants 83
Faith Festival 67
Faith+Vision 79
Family Films 84
Fandana Festival 68
Faunce, William H.P. 22, 23
Federal Council
of Churches 22, 23, 29, 42, 46, 48
Federal Council of Churches Committee on
Religious Drama 45, 46
Fellowship of European Broadcasters 81
Film 49, 70, 101, 102, 104, 113, 118, 120
Filmstrips 76
Fine Arts 13, 47, 53, 106, 107, 108, 109
Fine Arts Academy 107, 108
Fine Arts Department 106, 109
Fine Arts Series 106, 111, 112
Finley, Tom 82
Fireproof 83
FISHFEST 68
Fishnet '75 67
First Hand 66
Fisk Jubilee Singers 14, 58
Flag and Ribbon Ministry 108

Flinn, Randall 92
Floria, Cam 117, 118
Florida Boys 60
Flute 63, 107
Flywheeel 86
Folk 64, 65
Folk, Bessie 61
For Christians, Elves and Lovers 64
For Him Who Has Ears to Hear 64
Fortunato, Frank 120
Fowler, Frank 13
Frank, Kevin 82
Franklin, John 126
Franklin, Kirk 63
French Horn 107
Friends of Jesus 47
Frye, Theodore 61
Fujimura, Makoto 32
Fujimura Institute 33
Fuller Theological Seminary 101
Funk, Virgil 29
Gaebelein, Frank 32
Gallery 87, 101, 102, 104, 110, 111
Genesis Arts Trust 119
Gentle Faith 65
Gentry, Gary 67
George, Jeanette Clift 49
Geyer, Josi 97
Gifford Lectures 31
Giglio, Louie 69
Gilder, Jeanette 13
Girard, Andre 78
Girard, Chuck 67
Glimpses of His Glory Gallery 110
Glory 18, 26, 31, 52, 69, 94, 114, 124

Godspell 48
GodSpeed 86
God's Smuggler 86
Goff, James R. Jr. 59
Golden Gate Quartet 62
Golden Globe Award 50
Goodness 110, 124
Good News 49, 63, 94
Goodrich Gallery 110
Goodwin, Nigel 119
Gospelaires 61
Gospel Cartoons 82
Gospel Chimes 58
Gospel Ensemble 109
Gospel Films Company 84
Gospel Hard Rock 64
Gospel Music 60, 61, 62, 63
Gospel Music Hall of Fame 61
Gospel Music Workshop of America 61
Gothic Revival 73
Graduate Theological Union 102
Graham, Billy 30, 116
Grammy Awards 66
Grammy National Trustees Award 61
Grant, Amy 65, 67
Graphic Arts Ministry 113
Graphic Designer 103
Greek Revival 76
Green, Keith 64, 72
Griffin, Rick 82
Guitar 63, 66, 98, 107
Guthrie, William 91
Hair 48
Hafer, Dick 82
Halverson, Marvin 29, 78

Hamm, Jack 82
Handbells 107, 108, 109
Handchimes 108
Happy Goodmans 60
Harbinson, Colin 32, 35, 91, 125
Harp 57, 107
Harris, Robin 123
Hartford Theological Seminary 23, 25, 26
Hartley, Al 82
Hart, Trevor 103
Harvard Divinity School 23
Head of Christ 78
Hearn, Billy Ray 49
Heart Sound International 124
Heaven Bound 86
Henderson, Alice Corbin 67
Henry Luce Center for the
  Arts and Religion 104
Herman, Bruce 33, 79
Heroes of Faith 82
Hildebrand-Burnett Music Company 58
Hildebrand, Ephraim 55
Hills Alive 68
Hillsong Church 69, 107, 113
Hillsong College 113
Hip Hop 66, 94, 97, 98, 108
Historical Musicology 103
Hofmann, Heinrich 78
Homeland Harmony Quartet 60
Homily 77, 121
Honeytree, Nancy 65
Hopper, Stanley 27
"House of Love" 65
Hummel, Anora 94
Illustrations 27, 54, 77, 79, 80, 81

Index **203**

Image 83, 85, 122, 125, 126
Imagination 31, 32, 100, 102, 103, 113, 130
Improvisation 93
Incarnate 2012 124
Incarnate 2014 124
Interpretation 19, 32, 107
Initiative in Theology and the Arts 100
Installation 114
Institute for Theology, Imagination
and the Arts 100, 103
Institute of Sacred Music 103
Instrumental Insemble 109
Integrity Music 66
Interactive Parables 86
Interfaith Forum on Religion, Art, and
Architecture 76
International Arts Movement 33
International Association
of Christian Artists 118
International Christian
Dance Fellowship 93, 94, 119, 125
International Style 76
Internet 86
Jackson, Mahalia 61, 62
Jarrett, C.H. 47
Jazz 61, 65, 94, 95, 98, 111, 120
Jesus Christ Superstar 48
Jesus Movement 31, 48, 63, 65, 68, 69, 116
Jesus Music 67
Jesus Rock 67
Jesus '75 67
Jewelry 105
Joint Committee on Architecture, Methodist
Episcopal Church 72
John Benson Publishing Company 59
Jones, Mary 93, 119, 125
Jon Simpson Music 124

Jot the Dot 85
JourneyChurch 109
Joyce, John 86
JoyFest 68
Junior Partners Series 82
Kadey, Percy 78
Kaiser, Kurt 49
Kavanaugh, Barbara 69
Kavanaugh, Patrick 69
Kraft, Jim 69
Kraft, Mary Jeane 69
Keaggy, Phil 65, 67
Ken Anderson Films 84
Kieffer, Aldine 58
Kingdom Bound 68
Kingdoms 83
King's Fest 68
Kingstone Media 83
Kuyper, Abraham 17, 30, 31
L'Abri Fellowship 30
LaHaye, Tim 86
Lalonde, Paul 85
Lamb's Players 50
Landis, Tim 67
LaRiviere, Leen 117
Lathbury, Mary A. 14
Laurie, Greg 82
Lausanne Covenant 124, 125
Lausanne Conference 124, 125
Lausanne Movement 33, 124
Lavanoux, Maurice 18, 28, 75, 77
Lefevre, Mylon 64
Left Behind:Eternal Forces 86
Left Behind Series 85, 86
Letter to Artists 77, 121
Liberty University 68, 114, 130
Lifest 68

Lifetime Achievement Grammy 62
LifeLight Festivals 68
Light Records 49, 63
LightWorkers Media 86
Lindvall, Terry 83
Literature 23, 26, 31, 80, 102, 103, 104
Little Church Around the Corner 46
Liturgical Arts Society 29, 75, 77
Liturgical Dance 91, 94, 95
Liturgical Renewal Movement 28, 76, 116
Liturgical Theology and Practice 100
Lookout Gallery 99
Lord, Katherine 47
Love Song 65, 67, 69
Lutheran Church Art (later renamed
The Church Builder) 75
Lyric Religion 47
Mackaye, Percy 44
Magee, Harriet Cecil 25, 80
Maginnis & Walsh 28
Maher, Matt 69
Mainse, David 85
Makeup 54
Manila Manifesto 125
Marable, Eyesha 95
Maranatha! Music 65, 69
Maritain, Jacques 28
Mark IV Pictures 85
Martin, Roberta 61
Mason, Lowell 14
Mass for Young Americans 64
Mass of the Holy Spirit for Artists 77
Master of Arts in Theology 101, 104
Master of Arts in Theology and the Arts 105
Master of Letters in Theology, Imagination, and
the Arts 103
Master of Theology in Art and Religion 102

Master of Divinity 101, 102
Master of Theological Studies 101, 102
Master of Theology 101
MasterWorks Festival 69, 70
Master Works Touring Company 94
Matthews, Randy 65
McGuire, Barry 65
McGuire, Dony 52
McGuire, Reba Rambo 52
McKissick, Norsalus 61
Meiere, Hildreth 77
Men's Ensemble 109
Merlin R. Carothers 79
Metal 65
MetroChurch 52
MetroSchool of the Arts 52
Michel, Virgil 18
Mighty Clouds of Joy 62
Miller, Madeleine Sweeney 45
Mills, Anne 120
Mills, Jim 120
Mime 50, 108, 117, 118
Mind Garage 64
Minister of Creative Arts 52
Minister of Fine Arts 106
Minister of Music 61, 106
Missionary Education Movement 45
Missions 37, 44, 47, 72, 81, 97, 118, 119, 124
Mississippi Mass Choir 63
Mixed Media 108, 110
Modern ...19, 30, 70, 76, 78, 83, 93, 94, 95, 97, 98
Modern Dance 70
Modern Fusion 94
Modern Gothic 76
Moody Bible Institute 81
Moody, Dwight L. 16
Morgan, Roy 67

Index **205**

Morningstar 83
Morris–Henson Company 59
Moses' Rod 86
Movement Arts in Worship Conference 93
Munroe, Myles 105
Museum 26, 29, 78
Museum of Modern Art 29, 78
Musical Theatre 53
Music and Worship Studies 114
Music and Fine Arts Series 111, 112
Music Festival 67, 68
Musician 14, 29, 61, 65, 66, 67, 72, 117
Mylon 64
My Poor Generation 64
National Association of Pastoral Musicians 29
National Convention of Gospel Choirs and Choruses 61
National Council of Churches 29, 48, 76, 78
National Fine Arts Festivals 112
National Liturgical Dance Network 95
National Music Department 112
National Religious Broadcasters 84
Natural High 49
Neeley, Paul 123
Nelson, Hawk 67
New Artist of the Year 66
Newport, Esther 28
Next Generation Arts and Creativity 120
Niermann, Matthew 126
N'Lightning Software Development Incorporation 86
Normal School 15, 25, 57, 58
Norman, Larry 64
North American Conference on Church Architecture and the Allied Arts 75
Office of Franciscan Art and Architecture 75, 77
O'Kane, Tullius C. 14

Oklahoma Alliance for Liturgy and the Arts 52
OM Arts School of Mission 72, 124
OM Arts Theater 124
One Act Play 54
Online 87
Only Visiting This Planet 64
Oral Roberts True Stories 82
Oral Roberts University 52
Orchestra 53, 70, 106, 109, 117, 120
Organ 26, 69, 107, 111, 112
Organ Series 111
Ortmayer, Roger 30
Outdoor Drama 44, 53
Pace, Ernest 81
Pageantry Movement 44
Pageants and Exhibits Division of the Methodist Episcopal Church 45
Pageantry and Pictures 47, 80
Paradosi Ballet Company 97
Partnering 72, 98, 126
Pass De Deux 93
Passion Music 69
Patriotic Concerts 108
Pentecostal 19, 27, 53, 90, 91
Percussion 108
Performances 29, 39, 54, 92, 97, 100, 101, 111, 121
Performing Arts 69, 104, 108, 109, 120
Performing Arts Series 109
Petra 65
Philosophical Aesthetics 101
Philosophy 27, 28, 30, 31, 98, 100, 101, 102
Photographs 27, 79
Photography 25, 108, 110, 111, 114, 118, 120
Piano 36, 61, 66, 69, 70, 98, 107, 114, 120
Piano Performance 114
Pictures That Talk 81

Pius X School of Liturgical Music 18
"Place in this World" 66
Pitch 107
Plymouth Art Gallery 111
Podcast 87
Poetry Readings 104
Pointe 93, 98
PointFest 68
Pop 65, 66, 67, 117
Pope Benedict XVI 77
Pope John Paul II 77, 121
Pope John Paul XXIII 28
Praise '74 67
Praise and Worship Music 65, 68, 113
Pratt, Waldo S. 25, 26, 80
Publisher 12, 15, 58, 59
Premiere Festivals 67
Presbyterian Association of Musicians 113
Presbyterian Board of Publication 45
Preschool Ballet 94
Princeton Theological Seminary 17
Prints 102, 110
Project Exalt! 120
Protestant 13, 19, 26, 29, 45, 68, 76, 78, 80
Psalms in Scripture, Literature, and Music 103
Pueblo Revival 76
Quartet 58, 60, 62, 111
Radiant Dance Company 97
Radio Theater 108
Ramsay, Charles 82
Ray, Randolph 46
Reader's Theater 108
Readings 101, 104
Redman, Matt 69
"Redeeming the Arts: The Restoration of the Arts
to God's Creational Intention" 124
Reese, Della 61

Regent College 102
Reitz, Aury 96
Reitz, Tymme 96
Religion and Literature 133
Religion and Music 103
Religion and the Arts 33, 47, 101, 103
Religion and Visual Arts 103
Religious Drama Committee of the Drama
League of America 45
Religious Drama Committee of the Federal
Council of Churches of Christ in America 45
Religious Dramas 46
Religious Education
Association 22, 23, 24, 25, 26, 79
Religious Themes in
Contemporary American 103
Short Fiction 103
Renaissance 50, 125
Repertoire 51, 98
Repp, Ray 64
Represenational 78, 80
Resurrection Band 48, 65, 67
Rhapsodic Theatre 122
Rhythm 65
Robertson, Pat 85
Roberts, Oral 30, 117
Rock and Roll 107
Rock The Desert 68
Rock The Island 68
Romanesque Revival 76
Rookmaaker, Hans 18, 30, 41
Rouault, Georges 78
Ruebush-Kieffer Publishing Company 58
Run Baby Run 65, 82
Russell, Betty 82
Russell, Paul 51
Russell, Sheryl 51

Ryken, Leland 32
Saarinen, Eero 29, 75, 76
Sacred Architecture 101
Sacred Art 101
Saddleback Academy of Music 113
Saddleback Church 113
Saint Mark Episcopal Church 90
Saint, Phil 82
Saint Rita Fine Arts Series 111
Sankey, Ira 16, 17
Sayers, Dorothy 27
Sacred Art Show 52
Sallman, Warner 78
Salt '75 67
Saltworks Theater 52
Saxophone 63, 107
Schaeffer, Francis 18, 30, 41, 119
Scholar 17, 28
School of Communication
and Creative Arts 114
School of Divinity at Saint Mary's College 103
School of Music 103, 114
School of the Arts 92, 95, 98, 107
Schwartz, Rudolph 78
Scriptwriting 54
Sculptor 122
Sculpture 27, 78, 102, 108, 110, 111
Seasonal Concert 111
Second Chapter of Acts 65
Second Vatican Council 122
SEEN Journal 79
Seerveld, Calvin 18, 31
Sego Brothers/Sego Brothers and Naomi 60
Sequential 81
Set Design 54
Shape Note School 15, 57

Shekinah Dance Troupe 91
Shenandoah Normal Music School 58
Sherwin, W. F. 13
Sherwood Baptist Church 86
Sherwood Pictures 86
Shoemaker, Vaughan 82
Shorter Bible Plays 47
Sight & Sound Theatre 50
SIL International 126
Singing Convention 58, 59, 60
Singing Schools 13, 15, 56, 57
Skillet 67
Skit 48, 54
Slager, Julianna 98
Smith, Chuck 65
Smith, H. Augustine 47, 80
Smith, Michael W. 65
So Long Ago The Garden 64
Son of God 86
Sonshine Festival '75 67
SoulFest 68
Southern Baptist Radio and Television
Commission 85
Southern Baptist Sunday School Board
Architectural Department 75
Southern Baptist Theological Seminary 103, 114
Southern Gospel 58, 59, 60, 64
Sousa, John Phillip 14
Social Media 87
Society of Catholic Artists 77
Society for Arts, Religion, and Contemporary
Culture 30, 78
Society for the Renewal of Christian Art 18
Spanish Revival 76
Spradlin, Byron 33, 118, 126, 129
Speer Quartet 60

Spirit Song ... 68
Spirit West Coast ... 68
Stage Production ... 51, 97
Stamps–Baxter Music Company ... 59
Stamps–Baxter Quartet ... 59
Stamps, Virgil ... 59
St. Andrews University ... 31, 33, 101, 103
St. Luke's United Methodist Church
School of the Arts ... 107
Stanfill, Kristian ... 69
Star of the East ... 47
Statesmen Quartet ... 60
Step and Drill ... 108
Stevens, James S. ... 47
Stonehill, Randy ... 64
Stone Lectures ... 17, 31
StoneWorks Global Arts Initiative ... 32, 36
Stookey, Noel Paul ... 62
Street Theatre ... 50
String ... 70
String Performance ... 114
Stryper ... 65
Studio ... 61, 83, 91, 101
Studio and Digital Arts ... 114
Sturm, Bob ... 69
Sturm, Robin ... 69
Sudds, Karen ... 94
Sunday Pix ... 82
Superbook ... 85
Symposia ... 104
Surrendered School of the Arts ... 98
Sweet Comfort Band ... 65
Switchfoot ... 66, 67
Take The Message Everywhere ... 64
Tanner, Charles ... 49
Tap ... 94, 98, 107
Taproot Theatre ... 52

Taylor, Danny ... 67
Taylor, J. Mark ... 52
Teacher's Music Publishing Company ... 59
Team Ministries Contemporary
Christian Drama ... 52
Technical Arts Director ... 106
Telford, Mary E. ... 47
Tennessee Music and Printing Company ... 59
Tell It Like It Is ... 49
Terrell, Steve ... 50
The Archers ... 65
The Arts and Theology in Modernity ... 101
Theatre Arts Academy ... 50
Theatre Festivals ... 52
The Book of Revelation ... 83
The Brehm Center for Worship,
Theology, and the Arts ... 101
"The Bride" ... 52
The Brooklyn Tabernacle Choir ... 63
The Campus Christian Hour ... 63
The Caravans ... 62
The Christian Imagination ... 102
The Clara Ward Singers ... 62
The Columbia Institute of Fine Arts ... 107
The Continentals ... 117, 118
The Cross and the Switchblade ... 82
The Crusaders ... 82
The Dixie Hummingbirds ... 62
The Fairfield Four ... 62
The Flying House ... 85
The Gaither Trio ... 60
The Green Brothers/Al Green ... 62
"The Hiding Place" ... 50
The Hinsons ... 60
The Holy Ghost Players ... 48
The Hoppers ... 60
The Ichthus Festival ... 67

The Jesus Festival ... 67	Thomas, Harry ... 67
The Jordanaires ... 60	Thomas Road Baptist Church ... 53
The Kingsmen ... 60	Thompson, Donald ... 85
The Lefevres ... 60, 64	Tillich, Paul ... 29, 78
The Lesters ... 60	Tindley, Charles Albert ... 14, 60
The Life of Jesus Visualized ... 82	TobyMac ... 66, 67
The Liturgical Conference ... 29	Tomlin, Chris ... 67, 69
The Love Song Festival ... 67, 69	Tourjee, Eben ... 14
The Memory Verse Games ... 86	"Toymaker & Son" ... 91
The Next Generation ... 79, 120	Transform ... 97
Theofanidis, Christopher ... 33	Trinity Broadcasting Network ... 52, 85
Theologian ... 22, 29, 30, 78, 117	Trinity House Theatre ... 52
Theological Engagements with the Arts ... 103	Trombone ... 107
Theology and Imagination ... 103	Trumpet ... 107
Theology and Music ... 101	"Truth and the Arts in Mission" ... 125
Theology and the Arts ... 33, 100, 101, 103	Tuba ... 107
Theology and the Built Environment ... 101	*Tullus* ... 82
Theology Through the Arts ... 33, 100, 103	Union Theological Seminary ... 23
The Newboys ... 67	Unity Christian Music Festival ... 68
The Organization and Administration of Choirs ... 47	Unity College of Australia ... 119
	University of Chicago, Divinity School ... 47
"Theo-Rock" ... 64	University of the Nations ... 40
The Quail Game ... 86	University of St. Andrews, Scotland ... 101, 103
The Religious Lyric in Britain ... 103	University of St. Thomas Aquinas ... 101
The Resurrection Band ... 48, 65, 67	Unseld, Benjamin C. ... 58
The Resurrection of Our Lord ... 47	*Upon This Rock* ... 64
The Rich Young Man ... 47	Uprise Festival ... 68
The St. Paul Fine Arts Series ... 111	Urban ... 19, 94, 113
The Sensational Nightingales ... 62	Urban Arts Outreach ... 113
The Sunday School Times ... 81	Vagonova ... 92
The Virginia Normal Music School ... 56	Vatican II ... 122
The Wayfarer ... 44	Vaughan Company ... 58, 59
The Watchword ... 81	Vaughan, James David ... 58
Thibodeaux, Kathy ... 92	Vaughan Normal School of Music ... 58
Thibodeaux, Keith ... 92	Vaughan Phonograph Records ... 59
Third International Conference for the Development of Drawing and Art Teaching ... 25	Vaughan Quartet ... 60
	Veggie Tales ... 85

Veith, Gene ... 32
Verwer, George ... 123
Victory School of Fine Arts ... 52
Video ... 86, 87, 110, 118
Video Game ... 86
Video Streaming ... 87
Vincent, John Heyl ... 12
Vineyard Music ... 69
Viola ... 107
Violin ... 107
Vischer, Phil ... 85
Visual Faith ... 101
Virtual ... 87
Virtual Church ... 87
Virtual Reality ... 87
Visual Praise ... 109
Vocal ... 70, 112, 113
Vocation of the Artist ... 102
Walker, Tom ... 97
Wallace, Edwin ... 81
Ward, Clara ... 61
Warren, Rick ... 113
"Weak Days" ... 66
Weaving ... 108
Webber, Frederick ... 75
Webber Institute Center for Global Worship Renewal ... 123
Webb, Kathleen ... 82
WEC International ... 126
Weeks, Lee ... 83
Wendy Bagwell and the Sunliters ... 60
Wesley Theological Seminary ... 104
Wheeler, Ron ... 82
Whitecross ... 65
Wiggins, Kate Douglas ... 47, 114
Willow Creek Community Church ... 32, 53, 110
Winchester, Caleb T. ... 24, 25

WinterFest ... 68
Wisdom Tree Incorporated ... 86
Woodworking ... 108
Woman's Boards of Foreign and Home Missions of the Presbyterian Church ... 45
Woman's Foreign Missionary Society of the Methodist Episcopal Church ... 45
Wonder Jam ... 68
Wolfson College, Cambridge ... 101
Wolterstorff, Nicholas ... 18, 31
Word In Motion ... 96, 97
Workshops ... 52, 54, 95, 98, 104, 119, 121
World Evangelical Alliance ... 126
World Wide Pictures ... 84
Worship Arts ... 48, 113
Worship Arts Ministry ... 113
Worship Arts Pastor ... 106
Worship Band ... 69
Worship in the Church School through Music, Pageantry and Pictures ... 47, 80
Worship, Music, and Arts Ministry ... 107
Worship Team ... 69, 120
Worship, Theology and the Arts ... 101
Xaris Dance Company ... 121
Yale University Divinity School ... 103
Yale University Institute of Sacred Music ... 103
Young Continentals ... 117
Youth for Christ ... 67, 117
Zschech, Darlene ... 69
Zondervan ... 83
Zumba ... 98

Index 211

www.ingramcontent.com/pod-product-compliance
Ingram Content Group UK Ltd.
Pitfield, Milton Keynes, MK11 3LW, UK
UKHW022227230426
12048UKWH00016BA/1116